001.942 Cohen, Daniel
C

The world of UFO's

Child

DATE			
6 - 8			
9 - 13			
8 - 9			
10 - 20			
5 - 20			
7 - 6			
6 - 26			
9 - 29			
6 - 26			

PLEASE WASH YOUR HANDS BEFORE YOU READ ME AND KEEP ME CLEAN

© THE BAKER & TAYLOR CO.

The World of
UFOs

The World of UFOs

UFOs

Daniel Cohen

J. B. LIPPINCOTT COMPANY

PHILADELPHIA AND NEW YORK

The author is grateful to the following for help in obtaining information and pictures for this book: Jim Moseley, Gray Barker, George Earley, John Keel, Jim Oberg, Phil Klass, and Robert Scheaffer. The conclusions drawn in this book are entirely my own. Those who kindly helped me would not necessarily agree with all or any of them.

U.S. Library of Congress Cataloging in Publication Data

Cohen, Daniel.
  The world of UFOs.

  Bibliography: p.
  Includes index.
  SUMMARY: A history of unidentified flying objects, including accounts of several famous sightings and results of federal investigations.
  1. Flying saucers—Juvenile literature.   [1. Flying saucers]   I. Title.
TL789.0652   001.9′42   77–11659
ISBN–0–397–31780–8

AFTER SOME FIFTY BOOKS,
I UNBLUSHINGLY DEDICATE
THIS ONE TO MYSELF.

ABOUT THE AUTHOR

DANIEL COHEN, a journalist who was once the managing editor of *Science Digest,* has been interested in UFOs since he was a boy—he saw his first "spaceships" when he was thirteen. He is a member of the Committee for Scientific Investigation of Claims of the Paranormal, and often talks about UFOs and other mysterious matters on radio and television programs. He is also the author of many books, including *Magicians, Wizards, & Sorcerers; Curses, Hexes, & Spells;* and *The Body Snatchers.* Mr. Cohen is a native of Chicago and holds a degree in journalism from the University of Illinois. He lives with his wife and daughter and a collection of dogs and cats in Port Jervis, New York.

CONTENTS

1	MY OWN UFO	9
2	BEFORE THE BEGINNING	14
3	THE BEGINNING	21
4	ENTER THE AIR FORCE	28
5	THE 1952 WAVE	35
6	WHO'S COVERING UP?	42
7	CONTACT!	50
8	DANGER!	58
9	ENCOUNTERS OF THE THIRD KIND	66
10	KIDNAPPED	74
11	MONSTERS	87
12	SWAMP GAS	94
13	THE CONDON COMMITTEE	103
14	THE END OF AN ERA	110
15	OLD ASTRONAUTS	116
16	MYSTERIES EVERYWHERE	122
17	THEORIES BEYOND SPACE	131
18	NEW AGE PROPHETS	141
19	QUO VADIS?	148
	SELECTED BIBLIOGRAPHY	154
	INDEX	157

Chapter 1
MY OWN UFO

I SAW MY FIRST UNIDENTIFIED FLYING OBJECT when I was thirteen years old. That was back in 1949. UFOs were less than two years old then, and we called them flying saucers. I still call them flying saucers sometimes; old habits die hard.

I made the sighting in Chicago, where I lived. Chicago has a very special place in the history of flying saucers. Ziff-Davis publishers had their offices there, and Ziff-Davis published *Amazing Stories* and *Fantastic Adventures*. Both magazines were edited by the late Raymond A. Palmer. *Amazing Stories* and *Fantastic Adventures* were science-*fiction* magazines, but in Palmer-edited publications the line between science *fiction* and science *fact* was always pretty hazy, particularly in the editorials. Palmer liked to write long editorials, which he signed RAP, and they were often more thrilling than any of the stories he published. Palmer was always promoting strange ideas.

Palmer was one of the real pioneers of flying saucers. Many people, especially young people of my generation, had their first brush with the exotic and exciting world of UFOs through Palmer's magazines. Later ultra-respectable UFO buffs would try to forget about his contribution to Ufology, or at least pretend that it wasn't very important. But to me and to all the other kids who read *Amazing Stories* and *Fantastic Adventures*, Ray Palmer was the oracle on flying saucers. The fact that I was a regular reader of both magazines has a lot to do with the story of my own UFO.

One afternoon in the summer of 1949 I was standing on the

corner of Fifty-third Street and Kimbark Avenue looking up at the pigeons perched on a third-floor roof across the street. Pigeons always hung around that corner because there was a drugstore there with a peanut machine outside. You could never get peanuts out of that machine without spilling half of them on the ground, and that's why the pigeons hung around. I'm telling you all of this to show that I remember the scene vividly. I have forgotten a lot of things since 1949, but this incident remains as fresh in my memory as if it had happened yesterday. No, fresher.

I was looking up at the pigeons, who were looking down at the peanut machine, when suddenly above the third-floor roof I saw not one flying saucer but a whole squadron of them.

I was excited, naturally, but I can't say that I was surprised. Anybody who had absorbed Palmer's monthly editorials as thoroughly as I had really expected flying saucers to land at any moment—the only question was exactly where and when. Chicago in the summer of 1949 seemed as good a place and time as any. Perhaps they were going to land in Grant Park, and the little green men would troop over and present their credentials to Ray Palmer. After all, he believed in them, and most government officials seemed to be trying to ignore the whole business. He deserved to meet them first! (By that time Palmer had left Ziff-Davis in a dispute over flying saucers. He and Curtis Fuller had just started *Fate* magazine, which was to play an important part in UFO history.)

So there I was, standing on the corner of Fifty-third and Kimbark looking up at a squadron of flying saucers circling high above me. The saucers were perfectly round, a brilliant white against the clear blue sky. It was midafternoon, so there was no question of poor light, and my eyes were in perfect condition.

I watched the saucers for about ten minutes, with growing excitement. They seemed to be coming lower and lower. I was somewhat puzzled that no one else on the street seemed aware that a fleet of alien spaceships was about to land. People passed by and looked at me looking up, then looked up themselves, but didn't see anything that seemed to be of interest, and walked away. No one asked me what I was looking at, and I was too embarrassed to run down the street like a twentieth-century Paul Revere shouting, "The Martians are coming, the Martians are coming!" So I just stood there looking up.

As the flying saucers came lower, I noticed something about them that I hadn't observed earlier. They were *not* just round —they also had small wings. (That was the way I had seen them in some drawings—round ships with little wings.) I hadn't seen the little wings before because they were a darker color than the ships and had been obscured by the sun's glare off the brilliant white, round bodies.

The trouble was, the lower the flying saucers got the longer the wings became. And the bodies no longer looked round at all, but distinctly elongated. And the way the saucers were circling—there was something terribly familiar about it. Finally I could deny it no longer—my squadron of flying saucers was nothing more than a flock of seagulls. I was standing about a mile from Lake Michigan, and the lake near Chicago used to abound with gulls. I had seen them circling about high in the sky hundreds of times.

So my first personal experience with UFOs turned out to be a profound disappointment. I have seen a number of UFOs since. And I use the term in its strictest sense—Unidentified Flying Objects. I have seen things in the sky that I could not identify, and still can't identify. Perhaps the things I've observed were spaceships from other planets, which is what most people mean when they say UFOs, but it's more likely they were artificial satellites, bright meteors, or something else as prosaic. Though several of the UFO sightings I've made since 1949 were more striking than my first one, none have given me the same thrill. I suppose that's because that first experience marks the beginning of my disillusionment with UFOs. I had been shown, in the most forceful possible way, that the eye can be fooled. I would never have imagined that I could possibly mistake a seagull for a spaceship, and yet I had done exactly that. Seeing may be believing, but all too often believing is seeing.

I no longer expect alien spaceships to land at any moment. I am skeptical, and probably cynical, about any and all UFO reports, even from the most reliable observers. I have known too many of them to come to nothing. But that does not mean I have lost interest in the subject—not a bit of it. I have remained in touch with the world of UFOs for nearly thirty years, and I have kept track of the major sightings, followed the reports, the controversies, the conventions. I have read many of the UFO books and magazines, as well as stacks and stacks of little publications issued by tiny organizations or by individuals who insist that they have something about UFOs that they must tell the rest of the world. (I have a feeling that I may be the only person in the world, aside from their authors, who has ever read some of these publications.) And I have met many of the major and minor characters who have, in one way or another, been involved in the world of UFOs. It's been a hobby—sometimes nearly an obsession. And I have enjoyed it thoroughly.

I do not claim to be the world's foremost authority on UFOs. There are others far more obsessed and energetic than I. I also do not claim that by reading this book you are going to find a "solution" to the question of what UFOs are and where they come from. I am not even going to try to present a complete history of UFOs. That has already been attempted several times, with only limited success. Even a poor attempt would take a volume many times the size of this one.

This book is an informal history of the UFO phenomenon. By

informal I mean that I have concentrated on the incidents that I find particularly interesting and, frankly, particularly entertaining. I hope to convey some of the excitement, some of the fun I've gotten out of my thirty-year search for UFOs.

Some people get very grave about UFOs, or very angry. That is all very well for them. Perhaps it is the grim, no-nonsense technician type who will finally come up with a solution to the UFO mystery—though frankly I doubt it. In any case, that is not my nature. I lack the fervor of the true believer and the burning moral indignation of the rational debunker. I would rather sit down, relax, and swap a few good UFO tales, and that is what I intend to do here. So enjoy.

Chapter 2
BEFORE THE BEGINNING

THE MODERN UFO ERA BEGAN officially in 1947. Everyone agrees on that. But everyone also agrees that people have been seeing strange and unidentifiable things in the sky for a long time—at least since the beginning of recorded history.

Unquestionably the best-known ancient mention of something very like a UFO is found in the Bible. The object is the "wheel" seen by the prophet Ezekiel.

Now, what Ezekiel saw was considerably more than a wheel. It came in a cloud and a fire:

> Also out of the midst thereof came the likeness of four living creatures. And this was their appearance; they had the likeness of a man.
> And every one had four faces, and every one had four wings.

The description goes on into considerable detail, but it is impossible to get a clear mental picture of just what is being described. The story of Ezekiel's encounter with the "wheel" is one of the more obscure and enigmatic sections of the Bible. Nevertheless, UFO buffs are quite certain that what Ezekiel saw *was* a UFO.

An equally intriguing account comes from an ancient Egyptian document known as the Tulli papyrus. The document was said to have been the property of the late Professor Alberto Tulli, once director of the Egyptian museum at the Vatican.

The Tulli papyrus was purported to have been part of the court records of the pharaoh Thutmose III. According to the papyrus, the palace guards saw ". . . a circle of fire that was coming from the sky . . . it had no head. The breath of its mouth had a foul odor. Its body was one rod long and one rod wide. It had no voice." The papyrus also reported:

> Now after some days had passed, these things became more numerous in the sky than ever. They shone more in the sky than the brightness of the sun, and extended to the limits of the four supports of the heavens. . . .

This account is fascinating, but it is the sort of story of which one must say "interesting if true." *Is* it true? The tale of the Tulli papyrus has frequently been repeated by UFO buffs in books and magazine articles. But when researchers tried to trace down the document to check the accuracy of the translation, they ran into a blank wall. Professor Tulli was dead, and his belongings had been scattered far and wide. The director of the Vatican museum told the investigators that there was little chance that the document could be recovered—and besides, he doubted that it had existed in the first place. So there we are. But where is that?

Trying to pull UFO tales out of ancient documents is venturing onto very slippery ground indeed. Ancient accounts are full of hidden pitfalls—and so are accounts that aren't so very ancient. Take the famous 1897 Kansas calf-napping.

Back around the turn of the century, before powered flight had been successfully attempted, people all over America began reporting that they had seen "airships." The airships seemed to come in a variety of sizes and shapes, and they did all sorts of different things. What they had in common was that none of them could possibly have been built with the technology available at that time. UFO researchers now generally regard the airship sightings as a major UFO wave or "flap" that occurred before the term "UFO" was invented.

Probably the most sensational case of this period was reported by Alexander Hamilton, a prominent rancher from Yates Center, Kansas. Hamilton said that on April 19, 1897, he, his son, and their hired man saw an airship hovering thirty feet over his cow lot. The craft, according to Hamilton's description, was cigar-shaped and about three hundred feet long, with a large carriage under the hull. This carriage was "occupied by six of the strangest beings I ever saw. There were two men, a woman, and three children. They were jabbering together, but we could not understand a syllable they said."

According to Hamilton, a line or cable was dropped from the craft around the neck of a calf in the lot. Then, he said, the craft flew away with the struggling animal in tow.

The next day, according to Hamilton, pieces of the butchered calf were found in a neighboring field—but there were no footprints or other indications of how the remains might have gotten there. The obvious conclusion was that they had been dropped from the sky.

A local newspaper, the *Yates Center Farmer's Advocate,* printed the story of the calf-napping along with a statement attesting to Hamilton's honesty signed by five neighbors. The story did not remain local for long. It was quickly reprinted in papers all over the United States and Europe, and to this day it regularly appears in histories of UFOs.

Yet the story is a complete hoax. It fooled a lot of people for a long time. Skeptics, of course, never put any stock in the tale, but it is only fair to note that those who finally revealed the nature of the hoax were not skeptics at all. A complete account of the hoax and how it was born appeared in an article written by Jerome Clark for the February, 1977, issue of *Fate* magazine.

Fate happens to be the number-one American chronicler of odd events—everything from UFOs to ghosts. A cofounder of the magazine was Ray Palmer. *Fate* is a believers' magazine, but often a remarkably candid one. On many occasions the magazine has printed articles that the bulk of its readership could not possibly have liked. Clark's article was one of these, and I, for one, commend Clark and *Fate*. There are not too many publications that have the courage to defy the cherished beliefs of their readers.

The first solid information on the nature of the calf-napping hoax appeared in the January 28, 1943, issue of an obscure Kansas weekly called the *Buffalo Enterprise*. Just the week before, the *Enterprise* had revived the calf-napping story. That had brought a response from Ed F. Hudson, who had been the editor of the *Yates Center Farmer's Advocate*, the newspaper that had first published Hamilton's story. Hudson said flatly that the calf-napping had been a hoax and that he had been a willing accomplice in publicizing it. He also noted that shortly after the hoax there began a series of successful experiments in flight, "but I have always maintained that Alex Hamilton was the real inventor of human flight."

This obscure item was found in 1976 by someone doing a research project. It was sent to a British publication that specializes in printing accounts of odd happenings, and the editor of that publication in turn sent the clipping to Jerome Clark, who followed up on it.

Clark discovered that Hamilton and his cronies had been very experienced at making up stories. In fact, they'd met regularly as a Liars Club. Such clubs were a common feature of small-town life in nineteenth-century America; a bunch of the boys would get together regularly and amuse themselves by trying to top one another's whoppers.

A woman who had heard the story from Hamilton himself commented, "Well, to my knowledge, the club broke up soon after the 'airship and cow' story. I guess that one had topped them all and the Hamilton family went down in history."

The statement proclaiming Hamilton's honesty, this woman

said, was a phony; the five neighbors had signed it just to go
along with the joke. It must have seemed harmless enough—
and no one could have imagined that the story would be
around for so long.

In fact, Clark discovered, everyone around Yates Center at
the time knew Hamilton's reputation for extravagant tale spin-
ning, and knew that the airship story was just another of his
fancy falsehoods. But the rest of the world didn't know, and the
result was what Clark called "the biggest hoax ever known in
UFO history."

There is considerable reason to believe that the entire airship flap was based on a series of hoaxes—not organized or
malicious hoaxing, but just the sort of high-spirited leg pulling
that Hamilton and his friends enjoyed. Editors were only too
willing to print the stories if they would sell newspapers.
Hoaxes get into the papers even today, and in the nineteenth
century, when journalistic standards were much lower, even
reputedly respectable papers would knowingly publish the
most outrageous lies. But this airship business was going a bit
far. Even the publisher William Randolph Hearst (whose name
was once practically a byword for sensationalized and irre-
sponsible journalism) was outraged. He wrote:

> Fake journalism has a good deal to answer for, but we do not
> recall a more discernible example in that line than the persis-
> tent attempt to make the public believe that the air in this
> vicinity is populated with airships. It has been manifest for
> weeks that the whole airship story is pure myth.

Other newspapers also ridiculed the airship stories.

Not everybody agrees with Hearst and the scoffers that
there absolutely were no airships. David Michael Jacobs, a
historian from Temple University, wrote in his book, *The UFO
Controversy in America:*

Despite all the observations of the airship phenomenon and both serious and humorous speculation about its nature and origin, the question of what it was remains. Not all of the hundreds of consistent and detailed sightings can be dismissed as hoaxes, illusions, or hallucinations.

What is particularly intriguing about the whole airship flap is the way in which the sightings were interpreted. Laying aside for the moment the possibility that the whole thing was a hoax, let us assume people really saw strange things in the sky. They saw them at a time when the world was just about to enter the age of flight. Of course, people knew that experiments with flying machines were being conducted at that very moment, so they interpreted what they saw as "airships." Today, when we are just entering the age of space flight, we tend to interpret unidentifiable things in the sky as spacecraft.

Charles Fort, an indefatigable and eccentric collector of unusual events, published many accounts of sightings of strange and unexplainable things in the sky during his lifetime. After Fort died in 1932, there appears to have been a sharp drop-off in the number of sightings. That is probably simply because there was no one around to record them, not because people stopped seeing things.

The next major flap came during World War II. Allied pilots began reporting strange lights or ball-shaped objects hovering near their planes. These things were dubbed "foo fighters." The name is a pun on the French word for fire—*feu*. At the time there was a zany comic strip about a fireman called Smokey Stover. One of the recurring gags in the strip was the line, "Where there's foo, there's fire."

At first, some pilots were afraid to report the sightings because their commanding officers might think they were crazy. But after a while the sightings became so common that they were almost ignored.

There was some initial concern that the "foo fighters" were some kind of enemy secret weapon. But they never attacked or made any hostile moves, and that explanation was discarded. After the war it was discovered that German and Japanese pilots had been seeing the same thing. No solid explanation for "foo fighters" was ever offered, but the phenomenon was generally dismissed as being some unknown electrical effect or "mass hallucination." Today one of the more popular official explanations is that many of the lights were nothing more than reflections off the planes' wings. In the middle of a war there was no time to worry about unexplained things in the sky unless those things were obviously dangerous. No real on-the-spot investigation of "foo fighters" was ever carried out, and information about them is scanty.

In 1946 people in Europe, particularly in the Scandinavian countries, began reporting that they had seen strange cigar-shaped objects in the sky. These were dubbed "ghost rockets" by the press. At first there was some anxiety about them, because many of the sightings were made near the Soviet border. As soon as Germany was defeated in 1945, tension between western nations and the Soviet Union began to rise. Some people feared that the Soviets had developed a secret weapon. When that fear was overcome, however, official interest in the "ghost rocket" sightings seemed to die entirely.

The European sightings continued into 1947. And then on June 24, 1947, a very important event in the history of UFOs took place. It marks the beginning of the modern era of UFO sightings.

Chapter 3
THE BEGINNING

IT'S DIFFICULT TO UNDERSTAND why the Kenneth Arnold sighting on June 24, 1947, attracted as much attention as it did. The late Donald Menzel, an astronomer who for a while was the number-one UFO skeptic, contended that one of the main reasons was that Ray Palmer gave the case a lot of publicity in his magazines. In fact, Menzel contended that the whole UFO business was basically a Palmer creation. But Palmer didn't pick up the story of the Arnold sighting until after the newspapers had given it quite a lot of play. And Palmer had pushed other odd causes that had never caught on. There is some sort of mysterious chemistry about popular favor, but no one has ever been able to isolate all the elements.

Given the fact that people had been seeing strange things in the sky for a long time, there was nothing particularly spectacular about the Arnold sighting. Yet one must begin there. The details are so well known that I will repeat only the barest outline.

Kenneth Arnold was a Boise, Idaho, salesman and an experienced private pilot. He was flying his plane from Chehalis to Yakima in the state of Washington on June 24, 1947. In the vicinity of Mount Rainier he saw what he took to be nine disk-shaped objects flying at a fantastic speed. He described them as moving "like a saucer skipping over water."

The newspapers picked up Arnold's account and treated it with attitudes ranging from polite interest to complete skepticism. But whatever the attitude, the story did get a good deal of publicity, and one of those who read about it was Ray

Palmer. He asked Arnold to write an article about his experience; this article appeared under the title "I Did See the Flying Disks" in the first issue of the new magazine *Fate*. The style of the article shows that it was heavily influenced, if not actually written, by Palmer, though the details were the same ones Arnold had originally recounted.

You might note, by the way, that in the article Arnold called the objects "flying disks." The word "saucer" had been used in Arnold's original description of the way the objects moved, but the term "flying saucer" did not become universal until a bit later. (The terms "Unidentified Flying Object" and "UFO" came later still.)

It has become part of the lore of latter-day Ufology that Kenneth Arnold was an innocent who was swept up by "flying saucer" publicity. Well he may have been innocent, but he was certainly not publicity-shy, and he cooperated eagerly with Ray Palmer in promoting interest in UFOs. Arnold was Palmer's hired investigator on one of the most notorious of the early flying-saucer cases. (We will get to that shortly.) On the basis of the fame that flying saucers brought him, Arnold later ran unsuccessfully as a Republican candidate for lieutenant governor of Idaho, and for Congress.

The story of the Arnold sighting was the first of a flood of sighting accounts—some foolish, some not foolish at all. The public was already flying-saucer (or flying-disk) conscious by early 1948, when the excitement produced its first authentic tragedy.

On January 7, 1948, people in the vicinity of Louisville, Kentucky, saw a strange, silvery, cone-shaped object in the sky. Many of them called nearby Goodman Air Force Base, and when the men at Goodman looked up at the sky, they saw it too. They had no idea what it was, and decided to investigate. Three Air National Guard F–51s were dispatched to check up on the "thing" in the sky. In the lead plane was Captain Thomas Mantell, an experienced pilot. Mantell radioed the tower that the object was huge but that as he approached it, it sped away. He became extremely excited and tried to climb to twenty thousand feet to get close to whatever it was. He had no oxygen equipment in his plane; as he climbed he blacked out and the plane crashed. Flying saucers might have been a joke before, but after the death of Captain Mantell, no one was laughing anymore.

There was much speculation that there was something "mysterious" about Mantell's death. There is no real mystery about why the plane crashed. The only mystery concerns what Mantell was chasing.

What did Arnold and Mantell see? Neither of these two sightings would be counted a particularly good one today, but UFO investigation wasn't very sophisticated back in the 1940s. Arnold may have seen clouds created by wind currents from the mountains, or an optical illusion resulting from unusual meteorological conditions.

The Mantell case was more complicated. What the people around Louisville probably saw was a giant balloon called a Skyhook. At the time, the Navy was testing the balloons for use in high-altitude photographic reconnaissance. The problem was that the Skyhook project was secret, and though some people knew that a Skyhook was in the area at the time Mantell went on his fatal chase, they couldn't say anything. So the mystery continued for three years, until the Navy finally let the public know about the balloon.

Mantell himself apparently died as the result of his mistaking a bright star for some sort of craft. He started out on the trail of the balloon, but in his excitement began chasing a star. In moments of high excitement even experienced pilots make mistakes.

Many UFO buffs would not agree with these explanations,

but neither do they cite the Arnold and Mantell cases as the best evidence that UFOs are spaceships.

There is little disagreement about the next big case. It was a hoax that unexpectedly turned very nasty. In June, 1948, at a time when people were still puzzled, and perhaps a bit frightened, over the death of Captain Mantell, two men who had been fishing from a small boat near Maury Island, which is near Tacoma, Washington, reported that they had sighted several flying saucers. Ray Palmer heard about the sighting, and he sent Kenneth Arnold out to investigate. The men— Fred Crisman and Harold Dahl—supplied Arnold with another detail: one of the saucers had dropped lumps of slaglike metal on them and killed a dog they had had on board.

Arnold said he didn't know what to make of the whole thing. But he did think that something serious was going on, so he contacted Army Intelligence. Two officers from Hamilton Air Force Base in California flew up to Washington, questioned the men, and decided that the whole thing had never happened. The story probably would have ended there if the plane carrying the two officers back to California had not crashed, killing both of them.

An official investigation of the crash determined that its causes were entirely natural, but Arnold wasn't at all sure. He wrote, "Were both of these men dead long before their plane actually crashed, and is that the reason their plane was under little or no control?" Palmer hinted darkly that he wanted "no more dead men" on his hands. Rumors spread that the men's bodies had been riddled with bullets, and that a sample of the metal that the saucer had supposedly dropped at Maury Island was missing from the wreckage.

There was no basis for any of this wild speculation. The two men who had concocted the tale of the flying saucers admitted what they had done. They said they had wanted to make money by selling their story to a magazine. The government even considered prosecuting them. But since no one could possibly have foreseen the consequences of the hoax, the prosecution idea was dropped. An official report on the Maury Island story came down very hard on both Palmer and Arnold and the roles they had played in the incident.

Even in the face of overwhelming evidence to the contrary, Arnold remained convinced that the saucers had existed. He made a drawing of a slag-spewing saucer and included it in a pamphlet on UFOs that he later wrote. And Palmer went right on plugging flying saucers in his own publications. But both these early stars of Ufology were very definitely on the wane after Maury Island. Their identification with that incident may have helped push them into obscurity. There were new UFO personalities ready to take the lead.

And, naturally, the sightings continued. Another one of the early "classics" took place on the evening of July 24, 1948. An Eastern Airlines DC-3 was flying from Houston to Atlanta, with intermediate stops. The pilots were Clarence S. Chiles and John B. Whitted. At about 2:45 A.M., when the plane was about twenty miles southwest of Montgomery, Alabama, Captain Chiles saw a light coming right for the plane. Chiles alerted Whitted and put the plane into a tight turn to avoid the object, which seemed to be on a collision course. The men estimated that the UFO passed them at about seven hundred miles per hour.

Both men were experienced pilots, and they got a good look at the object as it flashed by. They said it had a fuselage like a B-29, but that its underside had "a deep blue glow." There seemed to be two rows of windows that glowed brightly, and "a fifty-foot trail of orange-red flame" shot out the back.

One passenger happened to be looking out the window at the time and he saw "a strange, eerie streak of light, very intense," but could add no details. Ground observers also reported "an extremely bright light" in the vicinity.

This case was far more startling than the Arnold incident. Here were two highly trained witnesses, both of whom had had a good look at something. And there was confirming testimony from others.

The Chiles–Whitted sighting is probably the only one of the early "classics" that is still actively debated today. Skeptics believe that this UFO was a bright meteorite glimpsed by a couple of excited pilots. But people who think it was a spaceship insist that such an explanation is highly implausible, because the primary observers were experienced pilots, not the sort of witnesses to become easily overexcited.

Another "classic" took place on October 1, 1948. Over Fargo, North Dakota, a pilot fought "a duel to the death" with a UFO. George F. Gorman, a twenty-five-year-old second lieutenant in the Air National Guard, was coming into Fargo from a cross-country flight. He had received clearance to land when suddenly he saw a strange light behind him. He called the tower and complained, and was assured that there was no other craft in the area. But the light was still there, so Gorman decided to investigate. He turned and closed in on the mysterious light, which neatly avoided him. Then it seemed to Gorman that the light turned and headed straight for him in an attempt to ram him. Gorman had to go into a sharp dive to get away. The light passed just a few feet above the canopy of his plane, after which it climbed and simply disappeared.

A shaken Gorman later told investigators, "I had the distinct impression that its maneuvers were controlled by thought or reason."

The case was an immediate sensation. And you can see why —Mantell had been killed, and Gorman nearly killed, because they "got too close" to a UFO. The things were very definitely getting an ominous reputation.

Yet it is almost certain that what Gorman was dealing with was nothing more sinister than a lighted weather balloon.

There are many other cases on record of pilots' carrying on similar "duels" with balloons. In one case, the Navy actually carried out a test with a pilot who reported that he'd been in one of these duels. The next night they sent up a balloon and had the pilot duplicate his maneuvers. The experience was identical.

Can a man pilot a plane and still not tell the difference between a balloon and a spaceship? The question really isn't fair, because night flying can produce all sorts of weird effects on a pilot's vision, no matter how experienced he is. Even hard-core UFO buffs now tend to accept the balloon explanation for the Gorman case, and it is rarely mentioned today in any list of good sightings.

But the balloon explanation for Gorman's duel was not offered to the public for over a year. In the meantime, the case only served to increase the confusion and the fear surrounding UFOs.

Reports of sightings, old ones as well as new ones, were coming in from all over the country by the end of 1948, and stories of the European "ghost rockets" were beginning to get a play in the American press. The atmosphere surrounding UFOs was emotionally overheated. It was unthinkable that some official agency would not step in and take charge of the situation. That task finally fell to the Air Force. It was a task that the Air Force was to regret undertaking for many, many years.

Chapter 4
ENTER THE AIR FORCE

IN 1969 THE U.S. AIR FORCE FINALLY ended its long and troubled official connection with UFOs. With a sigh of relief it closed down Project Blue Book, the last of a series of Air Force projects designed to investigate and try to deal with all the UFO reports that kept coming in.

Charles Corddry, the distinguished military affairs correspondent for the *Baltimore Sun* and one of the most knowledgeable of the Pentagon reporters, was asked what the Air Force had done in over twenty years of UFO investigation. Corddry's reply was, "As little as possible." That is as good a description of the final years of the Air Force investigation as you can find. But in the beginning the Air Force was not entirely disinterested in the subject of UFOs.

The late Edward J. Ruppelt, who was the head of one of the early Air Force UFO investigation projects, wrote:

> Although a formal project for UFO investigation wasn't set up until September, 1947, the Air Force had been vitally interested in UFO reports ever since June 24, 1947, the day Kenneth Arnold made the original UFO report.

Ruppelt insisted that in the beginning there was no question in the minds of the Air Force investigators as to whether UFOs existed. The only question was, Were the UFOs of Russian or interplanetary origin? The first Air Force UFO investigation project was code-named Project Sign.

Another reason for the Air Force investigation quickly

emerged—public relations. When the sightings began in earnest, different officials began issuing different statements to the press. Ruppelt called it "the era of confusion." And the public was becoming more than confused—it was becoming panicky, what with tales of pilots being killed chasing UFOs. The tension between the United States and the Soviet Union had intensified. Memories of the horrible destruction wrought by the atomic bombs dropped on Hiroshima and Nagasaki were fresh in everyone's minds. There was considerable fear that the Soviets were on the brink of developing their own atomic bomb. (They did begin testing atomic bombs in 1949, and that simply made people even more jittery.) The fear of immediate destruction was very real. To have people, and pilots in particular, panicking over UFOs was not going to help the situation—dangerous mistakes could be made in such an atmosphere. So an important aim of Project Sign was to cool down the atmosphere surrounding UFOs, as well as to investigate sightings.

Air Force General Carl Spaatz said, "If the American people are capable of getting so excited over something that doesn't exist, God help us if anyone ever plasters us with a real atomic bomb."

At the same time that the Air Force wanted to calm down the public, it was greatly concerned with secrecy. Today we have learned through a series of painful experiences that obsessive and totally unnecessary secrecy had become a way of life in the civilian government as well as in the military. The mentality of secrecy had been built up during World War II and never abandoned, never even questioned. Unfortunately, the public didn't know this. They knew the government had secrets, of course, but almost everyone assumed that if secrets were being kept, there must be a very good reason for keeping them. If something was being hidden, it just had to be important. In truth, most of what was being kept secret could have been made public without any problems. Often secrecy was a way to cover incompetence. And when it came to UFOs, secrecy often just led to more "scare" publicity—as it did in the Mantell and Gorman cases.

At first there may have been some legitimate reasons for secrecy. The Air Force never knew whether their investigation might reveal something that wasn't supposed to be known. For example, some Air Force investigators actually suspected the Navy of being responsible for UFOs. The Navy had experimented with an odd-looking circular plane, the XF–5–U–L, dubbed the Flying Flapjack. It never flew very well, and the project was scrapped in 1942, but some Air Force men thought that the Navy might have begun the project again on a super-secret basis and without Air Force knowledge. It wasn't until 1952 that the Navy officially acknowledged that it had once experimented with the craft, and released photos. That was ten years after the Flying Flapjack was dropped. Secrecy was an obsession.

And so it went. The Air Force investigators, never doubting the importance of military secrecy and, at the same time, hard pressed to issue quick, reassuring answers to the public, sometimes made official pronouncements on UFOs that had little to do with the truth. This eventually led to deeper public confusion—and suspicion. The Mantell incident was a case in point: first the public was given one explanation for Mantell's death, and then finally the information about the Skyhook balloon came out. Under the circumstances, it was no wonder people began to think something fishy was going on.

Project Sign came to an end in December, 1948, and the staff sat down to write a report; this was completed in February of the following year. The investigators were divided, some believing that UFOs were significant and extraordinary, others thinking that they were ordinary and hardly worth bothering about. The report reflected this split. But the Air Force investigators were nearly unanimous in the opinion that all investigation should be kept under strict military control and the investigations themselves kept secret.

After February, 1949, and the completion of the Project Sign report, the Air Force as a whole seemed to stop taking a serious interest in UFOs. Particular individuals involved in the investigations might be deeply concerned about UFOs—indeed, some even believed that UFOs were extraterrestrial spaceships—but officially the Air Force became engaged in a holding action, doing, as Corddry noted, "as little as possible."

Project Sign didn't really end; it was just renamed Project Grudge. But recommendations to expand the investigation were ignored. Historian David Michael Jacobs put it this way in *The UFO Controversy in America:*

> The Project Grudge staff tried to implement Project Sign's recommendations both by explaining every UFO report received and by assuring the public that the Air Force was investigating the UFO phenomenon thoroughly and had found no extraordinary objects in the atmosphere. Instead of seeking the origin of a possibly unique phenomenon, as Sign had done, Grudge usually denied the objective reality of the phenomenon. In this way Grudge shifted the focus of its investigation from the phenomenon to the people who reported it. Grudge also made a concerted effort to alleviate possible public anxiety over UFOs by embarking on a public-relations campaign designed to convince the public that UFOs constituted nothing unusual or extraordinary.

One of Grudge's major undertakings was to help in the preparation of a major two-part article on UFOs for the *Saturday Evening Post*—at that time one of the most influential of the mass-circulation magazines. The article came to the very strong conclusion that UFOs were all the result of mistakes and hoaxes fed by mass hysteria.

If the Air Force thought that this sort of treatment was going to end public concern about UFOs, it was badly mistaken—and quickly disappointed. The number of sightings reported to the Air Force kept right on rising, from 122 in 1947 to 210 in 1950. There was a slight drop-off in 1951, and it looked as if the issue might finally fade away, but in 1952 (as we shall see in the next chapter) there was a huge and alarming increase in the number of sightings. This prompted the CIA to get involved in the UFO controversy.

Just why the CIA, a spy organization, got into UFOs is not entirely clear even now. But the CIA got into a lot of things that it had no business getting into. The reason probably was fear that the Soviets might somehow or other use a UFO wave as a cover while launching an attack—or at least that the continuing UFO sightings were undermining public confidence in the military. What we do know about the CIA involvement is this: in early 1953, the CIA convened a meeting of selected scientists, Air Force representatives, and CIA men in Washington to discuss UFOs. The panel was chaired by Dr. H. P. Robertson of the California Institute of Technology, a mathematician and cosmologist.

The group met for several days, heard reports, saw films, and discussed UFOs. The panel members were not overpoweringly impressed by what they heard and saw. Robertson had to admonish one of the members for making jokes all the time.

In the end, the Robertson Panel came up with a report that said pretty much what other official bodies had been saying about UFOs for years—that there was no evidence they were a threat to American security, and certainly no evidence that they were spaceships from other planets.

Practically everyone agrees that the report of the Robertson Panel marked another turning point in the history of official attitudes toward UFOs. There is considerable controversy attached to the report even today. The main source of controversy is that the report was prepared under CIA direction. As we have now learned through bitter experience, the CIA has often lied to the American public. Not without reason, people have come to be suspicious about anything the CIA has had a hand in. The CIA says that it has no information about UFOs' coming from other planets, but people simply don't believe it, and that is understandable.

It is an article of faith among the majority of UFO buffs that the CIA knows something that it refuses to reveal. As I write these words, there is a strong rumor circulating among UFO groups that sensational revelations by the CIA are due "soon." But while we certainly should not take the CIA's assurances at face value, we must not automatically assume that the CIA is hiding information about UFOs. Some evidence that the CIA is, in fact, covering up something important should be produced. So far, none has been.

Another controversial thing about the Robertson Panel's report is that while it failed to recommend increased investigation of UFOs, it strongly advocated an increased publicity campaign to "debunk" them. It did not suggest, however, that any of the secret Air Force reports on UFOs be declassified—indeed, Robertson and his associates called for increased secrecy.

While the recommendations of the Robertson Panel were very much in line with recommendations that had come from Project Sign and Project Grudge, they seemed to have more far-reaching effects. By the middle of 1953, the Air Force brass did not believe that UFOs were either a Soviet or an extraterrestrial threat. (A few individuals may have believed differently, but they were a powerless minority.) The Air Force had no reason to go on investigating, and it might have dropped UFOs right there. But the Robertson Panel had concluded that UFOs could be a psychological threat, so it became the prime duty of the Air Force to get people to stop worrying about UFOs—not to try to find out what they were.

Apparently, however, Captain Edward Ruppelt, who was heading the Air Force UFO investigation project, then called Project Blue Book, was never told of the Robertson Panel's recommendations. Indeed, he seems to have been told exactly the opposite. He thought he was going to get a larger staff to investigate sightings.

But surely he must have suspected that something was seriously amiss when part of his staff was reassigned to other duties and no replacements were sent. All his requests for expanded authority were turned down. Finally Ruppelt left the Air Force in August, 1953.

Captain Ruppelt is one of the more interesting figures from the early days of UFO investigation. He seems to have been genuinely convinced that UFOs might be extraterrestrial spaceships. In 1955 he wrote a book called *The Report on Unidentified Flying Objects* in which he left the question of UFOs very much open. The book became quite popular, and UFO buffs have often used it to support the case for UFOs' being spacecraft. A few years later, however, Ruppelt put out a revised edition of his book; it contained three new chapters that brought the UFO story up to date. These chapters indicated very strongly that Ruppelt had changed his mind and no longer entertained the idea that UFOs might be spaceships. UFO buffs have hinted that Ruppelt was "pressured" to add those discouraging three chapters.

After Ruppelt's death in 1960 his book was reissued—without the three additional chapters. I'm not sure what all of this proves, except that books that say UFOs are or might be spaceships sell better than books that say they aren't.

Chapter 5
THE 1952 WAVE

WHAT CAME TO BE KNOWN in Ufological circles as the Big Flap occurred in 1952. (It was this flap that stimulated the CIA to become mixed up with UFOs by organizing the Robertson Panel.) And it was a *big* flap. In 1952 the number of UFO sightings reported to the Air Force rose to a whopping 1,501. It had been 169 in 1951 and 210 the year before that. This was a sudden, dramatic upsurge in sighting reports—the Air Force had never received anything like this many in a single year— and the 1,501 reports probably represented only a fraction of the sightings actually made. Most people just didn't bother to report UFOs to the Air Force.

The Big Flap began in June, 1952, and went on right through the summer. Air Force investigator Ruppelt recalled:

> To anyone who had anything to do with flying saucers, the summer of 1952 was just one big swirl of UFO reports, hurried trips, midnight telephone calls, reports to the Pentagon, press interviews, and very little sleep.

On June 1 radar picked up UFOs in California. On June 15, there was a flock of reports of a "silver sphere" in Virginia. On June 19, a fiery UFO buzzed a pilot over Goose Air Force Base in Newfoundland. On July 5, four hundred people lying on a beach in Chicago saw "a large red light with small white lights on the side" pass overhead, make a 180-degree turn, and disappear. Boston, Dayton, Fort Monmouth, New Jersey, and a host of other places were also heard from.

Blue Book was hurriedly sending its small staff of investigators from place to place. Some of the sightings turned out to be easily explainable as meteors, balloons, or other known objects. Other sightings did not fall into easily explainable categories, and excitement was building.

But what really made 1952 a year to remember in Ufological history was the flying-saucer "invasion" of Washington, D.C. Starting on July 10, UFOs were sighted in the vicinity of the capital. At first the sightings were fairly routine. But at about twenty minutes before midnight on July 19, eight UFOs appeared on two radarscopes at Washington National Airport. At first the objects seemed to move slowly, but then shot away at "fantastic speeds." They seemed to be moving erratically, in ways that no conventional craft would or could possibly move.

Radarscopes around Washington continued to track unidentifieds for several hours. There were also visual sightings. Airline pilots reported a variety of strange lights in the sky. Air traffic controllers at Washington National Airport spotted an unidentified blip on their screens just south of Andrews Air Force Base. They contacted the tower at Andrews, and when the tower operators looked out they saw what was described as "a huge fiery orange sphere" hovering nearby.

After the air traffic controllers got over their initial shock and checked their equipment to make sure it was working properly, they sent for Air Force interceptors to try to run down the "things" in the sky. But the Air Force was in no particular hurry to send aid. After several calls and a long wait, an F–94 arrived; it was almost daylight by that time. The crew searched the area for just a few minutes and went back to base without having spotted anything unusual.

If the Air Force brass were deeply concerned about the "invasion" of the nation's capital by UFOs, this concern certainly was not communicated to Captain Ruppelt, the man who was supposed to be heading the investigation. He didn't even find out about the excitement until the following morning. He arrived in Washington on a routine flight from Dayton, Ohio, and saw big headlines in the papers at the airport. He called Air Force Intelligence at the Pentagon but was told that they only knew what they had read in the papers. Meanwhile, the press was already becoming restive and hinting at some sort of Air Force cover-up.

Ruppelt became rather bitter about the treatment he was receiving. During this time of crisis he tried to get a staff car so that he could get around Washington more easily. This request got nowhere. He wasn't even given the money to rent a car—he was told to use the bus. Then he was told that if he didn't get back to Dayton right away he would be technically AWOL. "I decided that if saucers were buzzing Pennsylvania Avenue in formation I couldn't care less."

Angrily Ruppelt went back to Dayton, where he was pestered by the press. He answered "no comment" to all questions until finally his irritation broke through military discipline. When one reporter asked him what the Air Force was doing, he replied, "Probably nothing."

Meanwhile, all was not quiet on the Washington UFO front. On July 26 there was another wave of unidentified radar targets in the Washington, D.C., vicinity. Air Force interceptors were again sent for, and this time they responded more quickly.

The press heard about the sightings before the Air Force planes got there, and the radar room at Washington National Airport was filled with reporters and photographers. When two F–94s arrived in the vicinity of the airport, the press people were ordered out of the radar room. The reason given was that the procedures to be used were Classified. Ruppelt later called that reason "absurd." He insisted that the real reason was that some people in the military thought this would be the night that a pilot would get the first up-close look at a UFO, and they didn't want word to get out. Whatever the reason for the secrecy, all civilian air traffic was cleared from the area of Washington National Airport.

It was a dramatic moment, but the drama petered out. The radar targets disappeared. The interceptors flew around aimlessly for a little while and returned to base. As they left, the unidentified targets popped up on the radar screens once again. So more F–94s were sent for. This time the pilots did see some lights in the sky, but they were never able to get close enough to make any kind of worthwhile identification. When one pilot was closing in on a UFO he said that the light suddenly went out "like somebody turning off a light bulb." A couple of other pilots reported similar experiences. Actually, who saw what, and when, was not clear in 1952, and it is no clearer today. At the time this took place, Captain Ruppelt was out in Dayton, blissfully unaware of what was going on. Record keeping was sketchy at best. Things were, as Ruppelt later commented, "fouled up."

But the press was having a field day. Every Washington paper and many others throughout the nation were headlining UFOs. Ruppelt was brought to Washington, where he held off reporters with a series of "no comment" replies to their questions. It was an easy reply for him to make, because he really didn't know what was going on at that point.

And, apparently, neither did anyone else, because President Harry Truman's air aide called Ruppelt to ask him what was happening. Truman himself may actually have been listening in on the conversation, though he couldn't have learned very much.

The Pentagon and the Air Force were being swamped with UFO inquiries. It got so bad that all the telephone circuits to the Pentagon were clogged with UFO calls for several days. Things had obviously gotten out of hand, and something had to be done. So the Air Force decided to call a press conference.

The press conference, held on the morning of July 29, 1952, turned out to be one of the longest and best attended since the end of World War II. General John A. Samford, Air Force director of intelligence, was the principal spokesman, and he had several experts to back him up. The press conference was boisterous and confused, but General Samford did get his point across.

He said, "There has been no pattern that reveals anything remotely like purpose or remotely like consistency that we can in any way associate with any menace to the United States. . . . There is nothing in them [the UFO sightings] that is associated with material or vehicles or missiles that are directed against the United States."

What, then, had caused the sightings over Washington? Here the Air Force hedged, because it really didn't know. But most of those involved in the official investigation believed that the unidentifieds picked up on radar had been caused by a temperature inversion.

During July, 1952, Washington was having one of those heat waves for which it is justly infamous. Warm, humid air from the Gulf of Mexico lay over much of the southeastern United States. Above this flowed hot dry air from the Southwest. Such conditions are known as a temperature inversion. A temperature inversion could play havoc with radar back in 1952. The inversion would become more pronounced at night, when surface temperatures cooled down, making the contrast between temperature layers greater than ever. The visual sightings were also attributed to the inversion, for an inversion can produce mirage effects.

Not everyone agreed with that analysis of what had happened then, and not everyone agrees with it now. The Air Force itself first advanced the temperature-inversion theory tentatively. General Samford had not intended to present an "official" explanation for the Washington UFOs, though that is what it appeared to be to many. But as time went on, the Air Force became more and more emphatic in its temperature-inversion explanation.

Some of those who had at first reported impressive visual sightings began to change or at least tone down their stories when closely questioned by Air Force investigators. There were dark whispers that witnesses were being "pressured" to change their stories, but no substantial evidence of this sort of pressure has ever been offered.

As the excitement began to die down, other information was discovered that tended to support a natural explanation for the Washington UFO "invasion." During the height of the excitement one experienced commercial pilot had been told that, according to radar, a UFO was right in his takeoff path. He'd been asked to track it down. But neither he nor anyone else in his cockpit had seen anything unusual. The plane had made several runs over the spot where the UFO was supposed to be without seeing a thing. The pilot reported:

> Finally we were asked to visually check the terrain below for anything that might cause such an illusion. We looked and the only object we could see where the radar had a target turned out to be the Wilson Lines moonlight steamboat trip to Mount Vernon. Whether there was an altitude gimmick on the radar unit at the time I do not know, but the radar was sure as hell picking up the steamboat.

This pilot also dismissed the mysterious lights reported by others. He noted that there were so many lights around Washington that wherever you looked you could see a mysterious light.

Another odd point about the Washington, D.C., flap was that three overlapping radar systems were in use at the time. If the UFOs had been solid objects, they should have been picked up by all three radars in the overlap areas. But this only happened once.

The press played the Air Force "debunking" of the Washington sightings pretty big. And over the next few months there were a lot of stories explaining the whole UFO phenomenon as a mixture of mistakes and mass psychology. Whether the public bought these explanations is another matter entirely. While the Washington sightings marked the hysterical high point of the 1952 flap, people all over the country were still reporting UFOs well after General Samford's July 29 explanation and all the follow-up publicity.

By that time, the suspicion that the Air Force was covering up something significant about UFOs had sunk pretty deeply into many minds.

Chapter 6
WHO'S COVERING UP?

SURVEYS TAKEN IN THE LATE 1960s indicated that approximately 51 percent of the American public "believed" in UFOs. Translated, "believing in UFOs" usually means believing that UFOs are extraterrestrial spaceships. But when one survey asked this true-or-false question, "A government agency maintains a Top Secret file of UFO reports that are deliberately withheld from the public," a whopping 69 percent responded that they thought the statement was true. Among teenagers the percentage of those who responded "true" was even higher—73 percent believed the government was hiding something about UFOs. It would be hard to get that large a percentage of the American public to agree on anything. What is paradoxical about the survey results is that more people seem to believe that the government is covering up information about UFOs than "believe" in UFOs in the first place.

Such results are partly due to the atmosphere of suspicion that hangs over all government activities today. We have been lied to so often that it is hard not to distrust what the government says about any subject. But this feeling that the government is covering up something about UFOs is not new. It has been part of Ufology almost from the beginning. Indeed, there were times when people seemed more interested in *who* was covering up than in *what* was supposedly being covered up.

I believe that the idea of the great cover-up, like so much else in UFO history, started with Ray Palmer. Palmer charged "cover-up" in connection with the deaths of Captain Mantell and of the two investigators in the Maury Island incident. That was back in 1948. But Palmer faded into relative obscurity early on, and the conspiracy torch was picked up by Donald E. Keyhoe, a retired Marine Corps major, who carried it brilliantly for years.

Aside from having been in the Marine Corps, Keyhoe was a pilot and an experienced writer on aviation subjects. He had once accompanied Charles Lindbergh on a tour of the United States, and had written a well-received book called *Flying with Lindbergh.* Late in 1949, Keyhoe was commissioned by *True* magazine to write a flying-saucer article.

At that time, all the respectable publications like the *Saturday Evening Post* were debunking UFOs. (Later that was to change, for the subject of UFOs continued to hold public attention. Many major magazines like the *Saturday Evening Post,* faced with declining circulation, found that pro-UFO stories sold magazines.) But in 1949 *True* was not quite a respectable publication—it leaned heavily toward the sensational.

There is no reason to believe that Keyhoe deliberately slanted his article. Indeed, the rest of his career clearly indicates that he had become a true believer. There are times when he may have exaggerated for the cause, but like many others Donald Keyhoe was inflamed by the subject of UFOs. It became the consuming passion of his life.

Keyhoe had friends among the Air Force brass and apparently felt that he would have fairly easy access to UFO information. Instead, he came up against one blank wall after another. He got the feeling that the Air Force was deliberately holding back information that proved that UFOs were in fact extraterrestrial spaceships. He said as much in his article.

True editors titled Keyhoe's article "The Flying Saucers Are Real." It was published in the January, 1950, issue. That issue broke all sales records for *True*—a lesson that was not lost on other editors and publishers. Though Keyhoe quite clearly accused the Air Force of withholding important information about UFOs, his criticism was muted, because he did not know the reason behind the "cover-up." His speculations ran to what might be called "the *War of the Worlds* theory."

In 1938 the actor Orson Welles produced a radio adaptation of the H. G. Wells science-fiction story *War of the Worlds,* which was about the invasion of Earth by hostile aliens from Mars. The radio drama was done in the form of a regular news broadcast. It was very realistic, and some people who tuned in did not realize that they were hearing a radio play. They thought they were hearing a description of events that were actually taking place at that moment. Some listeners were badly scared, and there was genuine panic in the area where the "invasion" was supposed to have taken place.

If people could get so worked up over a radio play, Keyhoe reasoned, how would they react when they discovered that Earth really was being watched by creatures from outer space? Keyhoe speculated that the Air Force was covering up what it knew about UFOs to prevent a panic. Today, thirty years later, some UFO buffs still claim the alleged "cover-up" is intended to prevent panic.

Keyhoe expanded his article into a highly successful book. Ultimately he produced a series of books on the subject of UFOs. He also became the leader of the National Investigations Committee for Aerial Phenomena (NICAP), which was for some years the largest and most influential of all the UFO organizations. Under Keyhoe's direction, NICAP's members concentrated primarily on trying to pry out of the Air Force the important information that they were absolutely sure was being held in secret files.

Keyhoe's growing concern with the supposed cover-up can be seen reflected in the titles of his books. His first book, published in 1950, was titled *The Flying Saucers Are Real.* The second, published in 1953, was *Flying Saucers from Outer*

Space. By 1955 the question of whether UFOs were real or from outer space seemed to be settled; that was the year *The Flying Saucer Conspiracy* was published. It was followed in 1960 by *Flying Saucers: Top Secret.*

Keyhoe took "the cover-up" for granted, but he never condemned the entire Air Force, or even all of those involved in the Air Force UFO investigations, for it. Rather, he postulated the existence of a Silence Group within the Pentagon; this group, he thought, was responsible for keeping the important facts about UFOs from reaching the public, or even from reaching other members of the military. The reason for the "silence" was not sinister, but rather was a fear that if the truth were known panic would result.

Keyhoe was one of those people who had great difficulty accepting the general level of incompetence at which most large bureaucracies are run. It is now clear that the Air Force had bungled and bumbled and generally lost interest in UFOs, but didn't really want to admit it. Its "secrets" were hardly worth the effort. Keyhoe, however, could see nothing but conspiracy and cover-up.

Particularly ominous, in Keyhoe's view, was Air Force Regulation 200–2. This prohibited release of any information collected by the Air Force on a UFO sighting *unless* the thing sighted had been positively identified as some *known* object. Severe penalties could be imposed on anyone who ignored the regulation. Moreover, the regulation raised the security classification of UFO data.

Keyhoe and others frequently cited AFR 200–2 as proof that there was an Air Force cover-up, and at the time it certainly did look as if something pretty shady was going on. In fact, it now seems as though the regulation was aimed not at hiding any significant information, but at winning the public-relations battle with the UFO buffs. With every new sighting the Air Force, which was trying to cool down the UFO fever, took a beating, because bits and pieces of information—often wildly inaccurate information—leaked out. The almost instinctive Air Force reaction was to hold the lid on ever more tightly. But the result was exactly the opposite of what the Air Force had hoped. The tighter the security, the more believable became the UFO buffs' charges of cover-up and conspiracy. AFR 200–2 was a classic Air Force blunder.

The dramatic high point (or perhaps it was the low point) of Keyhoe's battle with what he perceived to be the forces of darkness came in February, 1958. A popular TV program called "Armstrong Circle Theater" was presenting a one-hour show on UFOs. Keyhoe was among those scheduled to appear on the show. Like most TV shows in those days, this one was shot live—nothing could be edited out of the tape later. Keyhoe had reluctantly agreed to read from a prepared script. But with the cameras on him he abandoned the script to attack the Air Force for withholding three secret documents. The audience at home never heard him, for the moment he stopped using the script the show's producers had the sound turned down—all you could hear was a faint mumble. But you could see Keyhoe's tense, angry face delivering what looked to be a significant statement. My first reaction was that something had gone wrong with our TV set. But when I talked to others, I realized that someone had indeed silenced Major Keyhoe.

Apparently the Air Force had nothing to do with turning down the sound. The producers didn't know what Keyhoe was going to say, and visions of libel suits danced in their heads. Live TV was always a bit like performing on the high wire without a net anyway.

The initial Air Force reaction was to deplore what the TV producers had done, because the brass felt that silencing Keyhoe had given his charges added publicity. Later the Air Force seemed to conclude that it really hadn't suffered at all, because Keyhoe had made himself look bad by departing from the script. UFO buffs, however, looked upon the incident as just another example of official censorship.

What about Keyhoe's charge that there were three secret Air Force documents? That was true enough, as far as it went. One of them was the Robertson Panel report. But none of the documents contained any hard information about UFOs. They were just policy statements that the Air Force didn't want released. Keyhoe had confused the undoubted fact of Air Force secrecy with the content of what was being kept secret.

Keyhoe had a tendency to exaggerate and overdramatize his case. Captain Edward Ruppelt, while he was in the Air Force, was certainly no apologist for Air Force policy. But after his retirement Ruppelt took Keyhoe to task for his description of what had gone on before the celebrated news conference on the 1952 Washington UFO "invasion." Keyhoe had pictured General Samford sitting in his room at the Pentagon debating with himself whether or not to reveal the "real truth" to the public, and then deciding that the risk of panic was too great, and that UFOs must be debunked. Ruppelt acidly noted:

> This bit of reporting makes Major Keyhoe the greatest journalist in history. He reads minds. And not only that, he can read them right through the walls of the Pentagon. But I'm glad that Keyhoe was able to read the general's mind and that he wrote the true and accurate facts about what he was really thinking, because I spent quite a bit of time talking to the general that day and he sure fooled me. I had no idea he was worried about what he should tell the public.

Whatever merit there may be to Keyhoe's theories about cover-ups and Silence Groups (and there seems very little merit to such charges), the cover-up idea has sunk deeply into the American consciousness, as polls taken more than twenty years after the charges were first made indicate.

Far more foolish charges of cover-up than those ever made

by Donald Keyhoe have also been making the rounds for years and years. One of the most persistent, and a personal favorite of mine, is the tale of the flying-saucer crash. As far as I have been able to determine, this tale started back in about 1949 with a man named Silas Newton.

Newton claimed he was a Texas oil millionaire, but he also happened to lecture on the subject of flying saucers. He said that a scientist friend of his, a rather mysterious fellow called "Dr. Gee," had told him that three flying saucers had crashed, killing all the occupants. A fourth saucer had landed but had flown away when approached by officials. The downed vehicles had supposedly contained the bodies of thirty-four little men from Venus. (In later versions of the tale, the little men became green.) According to Newton, the government had taken away the remains of the saucers and the bodies of the little men and were keeping the whole incident secret—in order to avoid panic, naturally.

Francis Broman, a science instructor at the University of Denver, invited Newton to lecture in his class—not because he believed Newton's flying-saucer story, but because he wanted to test his students' ability to judge evidence. The class unanimously flunked Newton's story, but no matter; the fact that he had "lectured" at the University of Denver got Newton a lot of publicity.

Newton had a friend named Frank Scully who had once been a columnist for the theatrical newspaper *Variety*. Scully wrote a book called *Behind the Flying Saucers* that was published in 1950 and was one of the first popular books on UFOs. Scully devoted much space to Newton's story, and denounced the government for covering up the truth.

As Broman's class had quickly seen, the story was a complete hoax, though whether Scully knew this or had just been taken in is unclear. "Dr. Gee" turned out to be one Mr. GeBauer, and both he and Newton were later arrested for promoting a worthless device for detecting oil wells.

Silly as it is, the story of the flying-saucer crash never dies. Hardly a year has gone by since 1950 that I have not heard another version of it. Once I was told that the government had the area of the crash fenced off and kept it closely guarded because it was so radioactive. I have been shown what was supposed to be a picture of one of the little men. I'm not sure, but I suspect it was a picture of the corpse of a shaved monkey.

In 1973 NBC was putting together a one-hour special on UFOs. Several people I know called me up to say that on this show the "truth" about the wrecked saucers would finally be revealed. The show said nothing whatever about the wrecked saucers from Venus.

And so it goes. I'm convinced that this same shoddy tale will be making the rounds a hundred years from now, and that there will always be people eager to believe it. It has been around so long already that it can properly be regarded as a piece of genuine American folklore, like the tales about Paul Bunyan.

Chapter 7
CONTACT!

ONE WAY TO REALLY IRRITATE a nuts-and-bolts UFO buff back in the 1950s or early '6os was to start talking about contactees —Earth people who talk to space people. The UFO buff would begin to growl that you were making fun of him and trying to lump him with "a bunch of frauds and lunatics." Then he might tell you that the contactees were really nothing more than part of the whole cover-up scheme.

It was perfectly respectable, in the view of the nuts-and-bolts buffs, to see mysterious lights, even to see entire spaceships. But if you started seeing the occupants of those spaceships you were suspect (at least until 1964). And if you began talking to them—that was intolerable, and it still is.

Contactees viewed the situation from an entirely different perspective. They weren't interested in what the Air Force knew, or in what the CIA knew, or in proving to scientists that UFOs were extraterrestrial spaceships. They already had all the proof they would ever need. They were interested in finding out what the "message" of the space people meant.

The most famous and most successful of all the early contactees was unquestionably George Adamski. In many ways he served as a model for other contactees.

Accounts of Adamski's background and early life are rather muddled. But we do know that for many years before either he or anyone else had heard of flying saucers, Adamski had been dabbling in the occult and the mystical. In 1936 he wrote and published a little book entitled *Questions and Answers by the Royal Order of Tibet.* At that time Adamski was billing himself as Professor; it was a title that was entirely imaginary, as was the Royal Order of Tibet. The book was fairly standard occult philosophy, meaning that it was hard to figure out. In 1946 Adamski wrote a science-fiction book about a trip to the stars.

But these ventures did not prosper, and when the UFO era opened, George Adamski was working in a tiny café near the giant Mount Palomar Observatory in California. He seemed to possess a genuine interest in astronomy and to have some knowledge of the subject.

As he later reported it, Adamski sighted his first flying saucer on October 9, 1946, nearly a year before Kenneth Arnold saw his flying saucers. Adamski wrote that he "actually saw with [his] naked eyes a gigantic spacecraft hovering high above the mountain ridge to the south of Mount Palomar, toward San Diego." The "large black object, similar in shape to a gigantic dirigible and apparently motionless," seemed to have "no cabin compartment or external appendages." As he watched, the craft "suddenly pointed its nose upward and quickly shot up into space, leaving a fiery trail behind it that remained visible for a good five minutes."

The following year, Adamski and four other people saw a huge flock of spaceships—184 of them by Adamski's count, though one of his witnesses counted 204. They passed overhead in stately procession.

Adamski took some photographs of his spaceships and peddled them about to various places. He began to lecture before small groups, and even published an article about his experiences in *Fate* magazine.

But the really significant event in his career came on November 20, 1952, when, according to Adamski, he made his first direct contact with the space people. On that night Adamski and six friends drove out into the desert in an attempt to see and perhaps talk to the occupants of spaceships. They were not to be disappointed. An enormous cigar-shaped craft appeared overhead. Adamski then left his companions and went driving off over the mountains.

He lost sight of the cigar-shaped craft but he followed a flash in the sky that turned out to be a small "scout ship" from the huge "mother ship" he had observed earlier. A short while later he saw a figure with long blonde hair wearing a shiny brown uniformlike garment waving at him from the side of the road. "Suddenly, as though a veil was removed from my mind . . . I fully realized that I was in the presence of . . . A HUMAN BEING FROM ANOTHER WORLD!"

Indeed, there was nothing in the outward appearance of this supposed visitor from another world to suggest that he was other than fully human. He not only looked human, he was "beautiful." Adamski and his space visitor communicated telepathically. The spaceman told Adamski that he was from the planet Venus, and that the space people were worried about all the nuclear explosions that were taking place on Earth.

Adamski was given a look at the "scout ship," which seemed to be constructed of a sparkling, diamondlike material. He got a glimpse of another "beautiful" spaceman inside.

Before departing, the space visitor told Adamski that a number of his kind were already living on Earth incognito, and hinted that occasionally Earth people were kidnapped by flying-saucer occupants.

Adamski said he had two cameras with him at the time. The spaceman asked to borrow one of his rolls of film, promising to return it soon (though it never was returned). With his remaining film Adamski took pictures of the departing spacecraft, but as usual he had trouble with his camera, and what he got was a series of blurry photographs that could have been pictures of practically anything.

Adamski's tales got a fair amount of local publicity, and with a British saucerologist named Desmond Leslie he wrote a book entitled *The Flying Saucers Have Landed;* it was first published in 1953. But nationwide fame did not immediately descend upon George Adamski—it took many more meetings with the space people, both on Earth and on board many spaceships.

The space people treated Adamski as a brother. They took him to view other planets, and let him in on the "secret" behind their repeated visits to Earth.

In "deep" conversations with the philosopher-chief of the space people, whom Adamski called "the Master," he learned that the space people were part of a benevolent galaxy-wide organization, and that they were attempting to keep the people of Earth from destroying themselves and from harming other, nearby planets. They had been at this thankless task for centuries, and from time to time they chose particularly worthy individuals on Earth to carry their message to the rest of mankind. Jesus had been one of their chosen messengers. For the modern age they chose—you guessed it—George Adamski.

The Master told Adamski:

> I think the peoples of Earth would be amazed to find how swiftly a change could come throughout the planet. Now that you have the medium for worldwide broadcasting, messages urging love and tolerance for all, instead of suspicion and censure, would find receptive hearts. For the great part of the Earth's population is weary of strife and its aftermath of woe. We know that, as never before, they hunger for knowledge of a way of life that will deliver them. We know that there is fear and confusion in their minds because they have seen and felt the results of two great wars that have served only to foster the seeds of another.
>
> So with receptive minds and hearts everywhere on your planet, it is not too late. But there is an urgency, my son! So go forth with the blessing of the Infinite Father on your mission, and add your voice to those of others who also carry this message of hope.

Adamski's book *Inside the Space Ships,* from which the preceding passage was taken, was published in 1955, and attained a degree of success unusual for such books. Adamski became something of a celebrity, not only among the already flourishing UFO contactee groups and the older occult and mystic groups to whom messages from distant masters were familiar fare, but among the general public as well. He appeared widely on radio and television, and, considering the utter implausibility of what he was saying, he managed to make a persuasive case. The National Investigations Committee for Aerial Phenomena and other nuts-and-bolts UFO groups hated his guts.

But I don't think it was Adamski's stories about the spaceships and the trips to other planets, or his foggy photographs, that formed the basis of his appeal. It was his message that superior beings who care about you are out there trying to keep mankind from blowing itself into extinction—which, as I've already mentioned, was a very real and very immediate fear in those days—that was so appealing. I don't know how many people really believed what he said, but an awful lot of people *wanted* to believe it.

Adamski's success spawned a small army of imitators. Truman Bethurum, for example, met a beautiful woman from the planet Clarion. Clarion, according to Bethurum, is part of our own solar system but we can't see it because it is directly opposite us, and therefore always hidden behind the sun. (That idea, by the way, was at least fifty years old. It had been used in a science-fiction serial called *Planetoid 127* written by Edgar Wallace.) Like Adamski's space people, Bethurum's Clarionites were walking about unnoticed on Earth, trying to keep the human race out of a suicidal nuclear war.

Daniel Fry, a mechanic at the White Sands Missile Proving Ground in New Mexico, was at work in the desert when "an ovate spheroid about thirty feet in diameter" came out of the sky and nearly knocked him over. Fry took a ride on the ship and learned that the ancestors of the spacemen had originally come from Earth. They were the descendants of survivors of a great war between the nations of Lemuria and Atlantis. These survivors had fled to another planet when Earth had become virtually uninhabitable. Now they were returning to save the current residents of Earth from the fate of their ancestors.

Orfeo Angelucci spun more elaborate stories of contacts with space people. But the basic message was the same: they had come to keep Earth from destroying itself.

Contactee Gabriel Green put a distinctly Christian slant into all his messages. His publication, *Thy Kingdom Come,* was more overtly religious in nature than most of the contactee literature of the 1950s. But Green also saw political potential in being a contactee—he entered the 1960 presidential race as the space people's choice. He dropped out before the election, but two years later he ran for the U.S. Senate in California and over 171,000 people voted for him.

Green also sponsored conventions, as did another contactee, George Van Tassel. Van Tassel's annual Giant Rock Convention in Yucca Valley, California, was probably the largest and best publicized of the many contactee conventions. Eventually a regular contactee convention and lecture circuit developed. No one became rich on contactee tales, but people could make a living at the trade.

Besides the contactees I have already mentioned, there were others—many, many others. Some were known nationally; most had only local reputations. While the big names in the contactee field would travel about giving lectures and repeating their stories on late-night radio talk shows, the lesser lights would stay at home, where they might gather small, cultish followings.

One of the funniest and saddest books I have ever read is

When Prophecy Fails, a report by a group of sociologists on the activities of a Minnesota-based contactee organization. These sociologists had infiltrated the group (not a difficult thing to do) and found that most of the small membership were young, well-educated, and quite intelligent.

The leader of the group said she was receiving telepathic messages from the space people. They warned that the world was about to experience a series of major catastrophes, and one of the first would be a giant flood that would destroy the city in which they were living. But there was hope for those who belonged to the little group. They would be picked up by a flying saucer before the deluge and saved from drowning.

So the little group (sociologists included) waited out in the backyard of one of the believers all one long cold winter night for the promised appearance of the flying saucer. Of course there was no flying saucer and no flood, but, oddly, the group did not dissolve after this severe confrontation with reality. Their leader informed them that the space people had said they were only being "tested," and most of the members of the group bought that explanation.

Ultimately the little group did dissolve, but for reasons mainly beyond their control. The sociologists concluded that the group as a whole was unskillful at promoting its message. But what if things had been different? The sociologists wrote:

> It is interesting to speculate . . . on what they might have made of their opportunities had they been more effective apostles. For about a week they were headline news throughout the nation. Their ideas were not without popular appeal, and they received hundreds of visitors, telephone calls, and letters from seriously interested citizens, as well as offers of money (which they invariably refused). Events conspired to offer them a truly magnificent opportunity to grow in numbers. Had they been more effective, disconfirmation might have portended the beginning, not the end.

It's easy to denounce the contactees as frauds; many of the nuts-and-bolts UFO people do exactly that. A couple of the small-time contactees actually went to jail for promoting a fraudulent scheme to build a flying saucer and bilking people out of thousands of dollars. Many contactees have been caught in lies time after time. Yet fraud does not entirely explain the phenomenon of the contactee.

There is a striking similarity between the actions and beliefs of the contactees and the actions and beliefs of the spiritualists of the mid-nineteenth and early twentieth centuries. There were plenty of frauds among the spiritualists. They faked pictures of spirits just the way contactees fake pictures of UFOs. But even the fraudulent spiritualists often believed at least part of what they were saying. They felt that the world needed some sort of dramatic proof that the spirits of the dead could communicate with the living, but they could not offer the proof—so, they cheated. The cheating was merely to serve the cause of the larger truth—a truth of which they were totally convinced.

What I am saying is that both contactees and spiritualists were often completely honest when they said they saw strange beings—be they spirits or space people—and heard voices inside their heads. I do not mean that either the beings or the voices were "real" in the sense in which that word is ordinarily meant. But in recent years it has become popular to theorize that contactees, spiritualists, and the like are in contact with "another reality." I am getting ahead of myself, though, because back in the 1950s Ufologists were still pretty much concerned with real, material spaceships occupied by real, material beings. Most of the big-time contactees shied away from purely spiritual explanations for the phenomena they were supposed to be experiencing.

Chapter 8
DANGER!

MOST OF THE MAJOR AND MINOR CONTACTEES had their space people preaching messages of peace and love. They were the benevolent big brothers and sisters in the sky. But there also seemed to be some evidence that the occupants of UFOs might be hostile.

The death of Captain Mantell and the controversy surrounding the deaths of the two military investigators in the Maury Island incident indicated to many that perhaps the space brothers were not going to be entirely friendly to people who got too close to them.

One of the early classic cases that led some to the conclusion that UFOs were dangerous was the case of the Florida scoutmaster. It took place on August 19 of the hectic year 1952. Air Force investigators had just begun to recover from the excitement caused by the Washington "invasion" when they received a sensational report.

A Florida scoutmaster and three of his charges were riding home from a scout meeting when they saw a strange light descend into a palmetto thicket. Thinking it might be a plane in trouble, the scoutmaster decided to investigate. He left the three scouts with the car and set off into the thicket carrying a machete and two flashlights. As he walked toward the light, he noticed a slight, pungent odor, and the temperature seemed to rise a bit.

The scoutmaster made his way to a clearing in the thicket, but he was becoming increasingly aware of the oppressive heat and odor. His breathing was labored and he had the very uncomfortable feeling that he was being watched. He took a few more steps, and then quite suddenly it seemed as if the whole sky had been blotted out by a large, dark, saucer-shaped craft descending silently into the clearing. The sight sent him reeling backward away from the clearing to a spot where the air was cooler and fresher.

He got a good look at the craft, which was gray and had a turret on top. For a reason the scoutmaster seemed unable to explain, even to himself, he was suddenly overcome by a furious desire to wreck the thing, though he made no move toward it. As soon as this angry thought entered his head the turret moved a bit and what looked like a small ball of red fire drifted out of the craft and toward him. It expanded as it came, and he was quickly enveloped in a red mist that knocked him unconscious.

The scouts back at the car saw it all. They became hysterical and ran down the road to a farmhouse. The farmer called the state highway patrol, which notified the local sheriff. A few minutes later a deputy sheriff picked up the scouts and took them back to the scoutmaster's parked car.

Meanwhile, the scoutmaster himself had regained consciousness; he was running back toward the highway when he saw the deputy sheriff's car pull up. After he calmed down and told his story, the deputy sheriff investigated the scene. He found one flashlight on the ground, still burning, and a flattened place in the grass where the scoutmaster had apparently lain unconscious. He could see nothing else, and the second flashlight was never found. Driving back to town, the scoutmaster noticed for the first time that he had minor burns on his face and arms and that his cap had been burned. The deputy sheriff called the Air Force.

A team of Air Force investigators—Captain Ruppelt, the Project Blue Book head, among them—were impressed by the story despite its rather bizarre details, and were inclined, at least on first impression, to believe what the scoutmaster had said.

The next day they went out to the area of the reported UFO landing and talked to other witnesses. "To be very honest," Ruppelt later wrote, "we were trying to prove that this was a hoax, but were having absolutely no success. Every new lead we dug up pointed to the same thing—a true story."

But then some disturbing information turned up. The scoutmaster had outlined his background for the investigators, saying he was an ex-Marine and a real solid-citizen type. That wasn't quite true. He had been thrown out of the Marine Corps for being AWOL and stealing a car. He had also spent time in a federal reformatory in Ohio.

The following morning Air Force investigators opened their newspapers to discover that the scoutmaster had hired a press agent and given hugely sensationalized versions of his story to everyone in the press who would listen. In the UFO-conscious year of 1952, that meant a *lot* of coverage. Though the scoutmaster had never been sworn to secrecy or anything like that, the Air Force investigators felt betrayed. "From all appearances, our scoutmaster was going to make a fast buck on his experience," said Ruppelt. The hunt for evidence of fraud began in earnest.

The evidence was not hard to find. The scouts were questioned again and major discrepancies in their stories began to show up. The most obvious was that they could not possibly have seen the scoutmaster hit by the ball of flame from where they said they had been. The scoutmaster's burns were of the type that could have been made with a cigarette lighter. More damaging information about the man's past turned up. One man who knew him said, "If he told me the sun was shining, I'd look up to make sure." The deputy sheriff who had called in the Air Force concluded, "Maybe this is the one time in his life he's telling the truth, but I doubt it."

The Air Force investigators classed the incident as a hoax. Most of those involved in the study of UFOs, including most believers, would probably agree with that judgment. Yet on at least three separate occasions during the 1960s I heard UFO lecturers refer to the case of the Florida scoutmaster without mentioning all of the damaging evidence that was turned up in the Air Force investigation.

Since those early days of the Florida scoutmaster case, a large number of similar incidents have been reported—cases in which an individual claims he has suffered some sort of damage, physical or mental, after a close brush with a UFO. I must hasten to add, however, that none of these cases has been thoroughly checked out, and many are reported only in a newspaper story or two, with little or no follow-up.

John Keel, one of the freer spirits among Ufological believers, asserts that he has personally interviewed a large number of individuals who have suffered grievously after contacts with UFOs or their occupants. These sufferings may be physical— burning eyes, recurrent headaches, that sort of thing—or mental—insomnia, nightmares, and, in a few cases, complete mental breakdown.

Now, one might easily argue that the breakdown occurred before the UFO sighting—indeed, was the cause of the UFO sighting. That is a reflection of the old "everybody who sees a flying saucer is nuts" point of view. But wherever the truth may lie, the idea that a close brush with a UFO can be physically or mentally dangerous has become part of the accepted lore of Ufology. There is even a hypothetical "contactee syndrome" with its own particular symptoms—burning eyes, insomnia, and the like—that people are supposed to suffer after a UFO experience.

An even more ominous part of UFO lore is what might be called the Men in Black (MIB). Many UFO buffs think that there are mysterious men, usually (but not always) dressed in black, who go around intimidating or confusing people who report seeing UFOs, or stealing evidence such as photographs of UFOs or things dropped from UFOs. The story goes that after meeting one or more of the Men in Black people often suffer from physical distress or extreme mental anguish (the contactee syndrome). This may sound foolish, but it is frighteningly real to a large number of those involved with the world of UFOs.

The first hint of the "existence" of these mysterious men came in the Maury Island incident. Before they confessed that the whole affair was a hoax, one of the witnesses said he had been visited by a mysterious "investigator" who had told him to forget what he had seen. At the same time the pictures of the "flying saucers" the witnesses had taken turned out to be badly fogged and spotted—as if they had been exposed to some form of radiation. Later it was rumored that the mysterious visitor had worn a dark suit, though that detail does not seem to have been part of the original story.

The incident that really made the MIB a permanent part of Ufological lore took place in 1953. Albert K. Bender was running one of the many small flying-saucer research groups that had sprung up in the early '50s. It was a tiny organization with headquarters in Bender's home. Despite its small size, the group was grandly titled the International Flying Saucer Bureau (IFSB). The primary business of the IFSB was publishing a little magazine called *Space Review.* The publication reached only a few hundred people at most, but these people were dedicated, hard-core saucer believers, and a high percentage of them were personally acquainted with one another.

You can imagine the readers' surprise, then, when in the September, 1953, issue of *Space Review* Bender published two strange announcements. First, that the flying-saucer "mystery" was nearing a solution (the common belief at the time was that there was a single "key" to the flying-saucer story).

Second, that the flying-saucer "mystery" had in fact been solved, but that the solution was being withheld by orders from "a higher source." Bender said, "We advise those engaged in saucer work to be very cautious." Bender then suspended the publication of *Space Review* and dissolved the IFSB.

Bender's friends and fellow saucer buffs were shocked by this abrupt and unexpected move. But Bender would tell them nothing. He did, however, tell a local newspaper that he had been "emphatically" warned to stop publishing by "three men in dark suits." Later, by some unknown metamorphosis, the dark suits became black. A lot of saucer buffs doubted Bender's tale about the three men. They thought he had suspended publication of *Space Review* because he'd run out of money. But enough did believe him to keep the story alive.

In 1963, a full ten years after he had dissolved his organization, Bender ended his long silence and wrote a curious little book called *Flying Saucers and the Three Men in Black.* In many respects it is a fairly standard contactee work in which the author recounts his many experiences with the space people. The work is also difficult, confused, and vaguely troubling.

Bender's first comments on the subject of his mysterious visitors made them sound very much like government agents. The theory of the government cover-up was strong in 1953. In an interview with his friend Gray Barker, recorded shortly after he closed down the IFSB, Bender was asked, "Why can't you talk freely about this thing?"

Bender answered, "Just before the men left, one of them said, 'I suppose you know you're on your honor as an American. If I hear another word out of your office you're in trouble!' "

"What will they do with you if you give out information?"

"Put me in jail and keep me shut up."

But in the ten years between that conversation and the publication of Bender's book detailing his contacts with spacemen, the theory of the government cover-up lost much of its exotic appeal to the wilder fringe of Ufology. Besides, others who had seen UFOs had begun to report encounters with mysterious men in black suits who had made veiled threats and taken away their evidence, and in most of these reports the witnesses had given the distinct impression that their visitors had not represented agencies of this earth.

When Morris K. Jessup, a well-known Ufologist, committed suicide in 1959, there were rumors, and at least one published hint, that he might have "ignored the warning of the dark trio." In truth, Jessup was a deeply troubled man who had more than once threatened suicide. There was nothing suspicious about the manner of his death. And to their credit, most Ufologists, even those who tend toward a paranoid view of the world, did not try to get publicity out of a personal tragedy.

In 1971 Dr. James McDonald, who had become the most energetic and outspoken supporter of UFOs in the scientific community, also committed suicide. There were few if any rumors of MIB interference here. Once again Ufologists showed a great deal of respect, restraint, and good sense— more than their critics might have expected.

More details were added to the lore of the Men in Black over the years. They often rode around in shiny new cars, usually black Cadillacs. (When they were reported in rural West Virginia, they were riding in shiny new pickup trucks.) Most often they had fairly dark complexions and black hair, and were sometimes described as looking like gypsies or American Indians.

In John Keel's book *The Mothman Prophecies,* there are reports of dozens of alleged encounters with MIB types. Most of these tales are not very dramatic, but they do convey a sense of the fear that pervades one branch of Ufological research. Keel reports that once he was phoned by photographer and Ufological researcher Dan Drasin and was told, "You know, this probably doesn't mean anything, but the other day I was walking through midtown Manhattan and an Indian took my picture. He wasn't even wearing a black suit."

Ufological researchers have ranged far and wide to find examples of MIB types appearing under strange and unusual conditions. Ufologist Jerome Clark even discovered a Man in Black in *The Autobiography of Malcolm X*. (Malcolm X, a militant black leader, was assassinated in 1965.) Malcolm was in a prison cell when:

> I lay on my bed. I suddenly became aware of a man sitting beside me in my chair. He had on a dark suit, I remember. I could see him as plainly as I see anyone I look at. He wasn't black, and he wasn't white. He was light-brown-skinned, with an Asiatic cast of countenance, and he had oily black hair.
>
> I looked right into his face. I didn't get frightened. I knew I wasn't dreaming. I couldn't move, I didn't speak, and he didn't. I couldn't place him racially—other than I knew he was non-European. I had no idea whatsoever who he was. He just sat there. Then, suddenly as he had come, he was gone.

I don't know what Malcolm X saw, or thought he saw. I don't even know what he meant by including this strange passage in his book. But I do know what the Ufologists mean when they point to it; they mean, "Watch out! The MIB are everywhere!"

Chapter 9
ENCOUNTERS OF THE THIRD KIND

THE PHRASE I HAVE USED for the title of this chapter, "encounters of the third kind," was coined by Dr. J. Allen Hynek, an astronomer from Northwestern University who has been associated with the investigation of UFOs longer than any other scientist. It is also part of the title of a major motion picture about UFOs. What it means is close-up UFO sightings in which the occupants of the UFOs were also seen.

At the beginning of Chapter 7 I said that during the 1950s and early '60s the nuts-and-bolts UFO buffs tended to disregard anyone who said he or she had seen the occupants of spaceships. But during the past ten years or so that position has softened. Not that attitudes toward contactees have changed. It may be okay in this day and age to *see* the occupants of UFOs, but talking to them is still pretty much taboo.

The best early example of an "encounter of the third kind" took place in New Guinea in June, 1959. One of Hynek's close associates, French-born mathematician Jacques Vallee, calls it "one of the great classics in UFO history" in his book *Anatomy of a Phenomenon.*

In June, 1959, the Reverend William Booth Gill, an Anglican missionary, was living in Papua, one of the remote areas in already remote New Guinea. That month Reverend Gill and thirty-seven of the natives attached to his mission watched a large saucerlike craft hovering three to four hundred feet off the ground. They could see four men on what seemed to be "a deck on top of the huge disk." Reverend Gill waved and "all four figures waved back."

This is a first-rate sighting—if it could be adequately documented. But there, alas, is the rub. Vallee says the sighting "has a perfectly official character and has remained unidentified after a number of investigations." But the only source he cites is *The Australian Flying Saucer Review.* The incident has been mentioned in a large number of other UFO books, but none supplies any details about the investigations that were supposed to have been made at the time.

In a review I wrote of *Anatomy of a Phenomenon,* I complained about the fact that Vallee gave no source of information on the alleged investigations other than *The Australian Flying Saucer Review*—which, after all, is not readily available to many people. The complaint stimulated about a dozen letters from UFO buffs who insisted that there was "lots of documentation." But no one could seem to remember where it was. I was even sent what was supposed to be a copy of a letter written by Reverend Gill himself, which stated that he did see what he said he saw, and he couldn't understand it any better than the next fellow, and he certainly wished that someone would explain it to him someday.

A persistent problem with sightings reported in distant places is that they are almost impossible to check out in any adequate manner. Yet they are frequently trotted out as "proof" that UFOs are spaceships.

The 1959 Papua sighting became so famous that eventually Dr. Hynek himself traveled all the way to New Guinea to investigate it. He also met with Reverend Gill, who was in Australia at the time. Hynek could add no new material evidence to the case, but reported that he had found Reverend Gill a truthful man, and not the sort who would contrive a hoax. But skeptics point out oddities in Reverend Gill's story that lead them to suspect he's not so truthful after all. Why, for example, did he go in for dinner in the middle of the sighting, as he said he did?

The first American sighting of a spacecraft and its occupants to attract serious attention was the Socorro, New Mexico, incident. The witnesses' account goes like this:

Late in the afternoon of April 24, 1964, Deputy Marshal Lonnie Zamora was chasing a speeder when he heard a roar and saw flames to his right. Thinking a dynamite shack in the area had exploded, Zamora abandoned his chase and turned off in the direction of the shack. Looking over the hilly desert landscape, Zamora saw not a burning dynamite shack but a shiny object that he first took to be an overturned car. But as he drew closer he realized that what he was looking at was an egg-shaped spacecraft with two people in white coveralls standing near it. When they saw him they seemed startled. Zamora radioed the sheriff's office, because he was getting scared.

He stopped his car about one hundred feet from the craft and got out. As he did, a roar and a bluish flame issued from the craft, and it began to rise into the air. This frightened Zamora even more; he started to run back toward his car but bumped into it, and his glasses fell off. He then ducked to the ground and covered his head with his hands, and thus was unable to see the craft depart.

When he had recovered his equilibrium a bit, Zamora again got on the radio and asked the radio dispatcher to look out his window to see if he could spot the object. The dispatcher couldn't.

Zamora went to the area where the craft had been. He saw some burning vegetation and four small depressions in the ground. The sheriff arrived within minutes and found Zamora still looking badly shaken. The sheriff also checked the "landing area" and noted the burns and indentations. Later, one confirming witness was reported—a gas-station attendant who said that just before the sighting an unidentified motorist told him he had seen a silvery object headed toward the area where Zamora saw the egg-shaped craft.

This incident got a good deal of publicity, mainly because Zamora, unlike the Florida scoutmaster, was a man of excellent reputation. So the Air Force sent Dr. Hynek down to investigate.

Hynek had been an Air Force consultant on UFOs since the early days of the Air Force investigation. For some years he had privately believed that there was more to the UFO problem than the official Air Force position would allow. Though his opinions were well known to his friends, he hesitated to discuss them in public.

Hynek went down to New Mexico and talked to Zamora, who by that time was a veteran at being interviewed—he had already told his story to a host of other investigators, official and unofficial. Hynek was impressed with the man, and in a widely circulated statement he said that Zamora was "basically sincere, honest, and reliable. He would not be capable of contriving a complex hoax, nor would his temperament indicate that he would have the slightest interest in such." Hynek's report ruled out hallucination, noted that Zamora was a nondrinking man, and concluded:

> . . . Zamora saw a tangible, physical object, under good daylight illumination, and from fairly close range (at closest almost as little as one hundred feet). It appears essential that we discover what the physical object actually was . . . [and] consider this one of the major UFO sightings in the history of the Air Force's consideration of this subject. . . . It would require, very possibly, the attention of the Secretary of the Air Force himself.

Hynek's report was not an official Air Force judgment on what Zamora saw, but the general public tended to see it that way. It sounded a great deal as if Air Force scientists had decided that Lonnie Zamora had actually seen a spaceship and two alien beings. Officially the Air Force listed the case as unidentified, making it the only combination landing, trace, and occupant case listed as unidentified in the files of Project Blue Book. (A "trace" case is one in which physical evidence was left—in this case the burning vegetation and depressions in the ground.)

The case attracted the attention of NICAP and other, more respectable and orthodox Ufological groups. They had always been leery of occupant cases because they were just a bit too similar to contactee cases. But this incident caused them to rethink their position.

Not everyone believed Lonnie Zamora's story, of course. In 1966 Phil Klass became interested in the case. Klass was (and is) an editor for the prestigious technical publication *Aviation Week and Space Technology.* He had become intrigued by some UFO sightings and had developed a theory that he believed accounted for them. He wrote an article explaining his theory and received a good deal of publicity—as well as a lot of hostile reaction from UFO buffs. Being combative by nature, he took up other cases, and quickly got himself a reputation as the arch-UFO skeptic—a reputation he still has today.

Klass went down to Socorro, talked to Zamora, investigated the site of the alleged landing, and came up with what he regarded as extremely troubling discrepancies in Zamora's story. His objections are fairly detailed, but the two major ones are that from where Zamora said he was when he first saw the craft and the two beings, it would have been very difficult for him to see anything very clearly; and that there was a house nearby and the people in it should have seen the craft, or at least heard the noise it made, for Zamora described the noise as being very loud. But the people heard and saw nothing.

Why did Zamora say that he had seen a spaceship if he had not? Perhaps he was just trying to help out his community. Klass found evidence that the people in Socorro intended to use publicity about the landing to promote tourism to the area. Indeed, by 1966 they had already improved the road to the spot where the landing was said to have taken place.

UFO buffs, who are deeply committed to the truth of the Zamora case, have raised objections to Klass's objections. Jim and Coral Lorenzen, joint heads of the Aerial Phenomena Research Organization (APRO), one of the oldest and most stable of the UFO groups, were particularly involved with Socorro and particularly incensed by Klass. They have written:

> We personally think that Phil Klass is "putting us on" and having a good laugh (all the way to the bank) at the expense of us "buffs" whom he scorns and that portion of the reading public that is taken in by his pseudoscience.

One of the most recent of the classic "encounters of the third kind" took place in 1975 near Fort Lee, New Jersey, just across the river from New York City. In mid-January George O'Barski, a seventy-three-year-old liquor salesman, was driving home from work late at night when he saw what looked to him like a round spaceship land in a grassy area near the Stonehenge apartment complex. He was less than a hundred feet away, he said, and he watched small-statured beings climb out of the spaceship, apparently collect soil samples, and then get back into their ship and fly away. The following day O'Barski found small holes in the ground where the UFO occupants had been seen digging.

O'Barski didn't make any great fuss about his sighting; he didn't seem to want publicity (though he didn't avoid it either). There certainly could have been no possible plan to turn the Stonehenge apartments into a tourist attraction. But he did tell a few people; word got out, and the story was eventually picked up by the newspapers and covered on New York City television.

Early in 1977 I met O'Barski and heard him recount his experience, and frankly it is difficult to argue with the man. He is a perfectly straightforward and unassuming person. He asserts that he never had an experience like that before and has

not had one since. He has no idea what happened, and rather
wishes that it hadn't. In short, the man sounds down-to-earth
—and dead honest. Yet it is almost impossible to believe what
he says.

For a spaceship to land in one of the most heavily urbanized
areas in the entire world and be seen by only one person seems
out of the question. Some UFO investigators claim that they
have found other witnesses to the landing, but so far only one
of these witnesses has been identified, and his story is vague.
And even taking all the rumors of additional observers into
account, there still are not nearly enough witnesses to make
the story credible.

How is one to deal with a tale like George O'Barski's? It is
really one man's word, and no matter how straightforward and
honest he sounds, it is still only one man's word. That is just not
good enough.

The incident has a rather foolish and funny postscript. The
alleged landing took place near the home of Jim Moseley, one
of the early luminaries among UFO buffs. Moseley was asked
to arrange a sort of "saucer seance" at which Warren and
Libby Freiberg, a couple of Chicago contactee-mediums, were
to try to get in touch with the space people. This seance would
take place at a spot near the alleged landing site.

Moseley is a representative of what has been called Middle
Ufology—that is, he is willing to entertain practically any idea
about UFOs, and he has a lot of fun at it (though he is serious
in his beliefs). So he helped set up the seance. But it turned out
to be much more than he had bargained for. He wrote:

> Little did we know that the local press would release the time
> and location of the event ahead of time. At North Hudson Park
> [where the UFO was supposed to have landed], we were met
> not only by the media but by MUFON representatives
> [MUFON is an organization of UFO buffs], cultists, and a mob

of about five hundred people, mostly teenagers out for a good time on Saturday night. In spite of the somewhat hostile crowd, the Freibergs bravely went out into the "landing field." We formed a circle around them, chanting, at their request, "Alpha, Omega." From the mob came a rival chant of "Frisbee, Frisbee," and other unharmonious phrases. Eventually the noise level became intolerable. At just about the time that the crowd was closing in heavily around the Freibergs, everyone's attention was diverted to the distant sight of a midget or child in a tinfoil outfit, carrying a flare. As the crowd rushed off to investigate, a few of us headed in the opposite direction, to regroup in the foyer of Stonehenge. But then, as soon as the "spaceman" ran off into the night, the mob spotted the Freibergs getting into their automobile. They rushed over and started pounding on the car and rocking it. The psychic pair was lucky to get out of the park unhurt!

A few minutes later a seance was held on the roof of the Stonehenge apartments. The Freibergs claimed to have contacted a people called the Grapalins who promised to appear over Times Square on the night of July 4, 1976, in honor of the American Bicentennial. It never happened.

Chapter 10
KIDNAPPED

GEORGE O'BARSKI SAID that he saw the little men from the flying saucer digging up soil samples. Is it possible that Ufonauts have been taking other kinds of samples—like people? A number of famous cases hint at that alarming conclusion, and we will look at some of them.

Unquestionably the best-known case is the Betty and Barney Hill incident. It has been the subject of a popular book, *The Interrupted Journey*, by John Fuller, and the book was made into quite a good TV movie shown nationwide in 1976. As described in the book and movie, the facts of the case go like this:

The Hills were driving back to their home in Portsmouth, New Hampshire, from Montreal, Canada, on the night of September 19, 1961. They were going through a deserted area in the White Mountains when their attention was attracted by a bright object that seemed to be following their car. Barney Hill became alarmed, stopped the car, got out, and looked at the object through binoculars. It looked to him like a spaceship with alien faces peering out through the windows. He ran back to the car in a near panic. The Hills drove off, but the next several hours were blank in both their memories. Furthermore, when they "came to" again they found that they had not progressed as far down the road as they should have. There were several "lost hours" on the trip.

When they returned home, Betty Hill was troubled by nightmares, and Barney had headaches and other symptoms. Finally they contacted a prominent Boston psychiatrist, Dr. Benjamin Simon. Under hypnosis the Hills separately told similar stories of being stopped on the road by alien creatures, taken aboard a spaceship, subjected to a thorough and somewhat humiliating physical examination, and then being released. Under posthypnotic suggestion Barney drew pictures of the creatures he said had abducted him. Betty drew a "star map" that she said she had seen aboard the UFO. The map was said to perfectly match the patterns of certain stars.

Now, it must be said at the outset that there is not a scrap of confirming evidence, aside from the testimony of the Hills themselves, that any of this ever happened. The fame of the case rests, in large measure, on the character of the two witnesses. They were both intelligent, upstanding people who were not publicity seekers; indeed, at first they sought to avoid publicity.

I met Betty Hill briefly in 1977 (Barney had died a few years earlier). I talked to her and heard her tell the story of her "abduction." In the world of UFO contactees Betty Hill is a star, and deservedly so. Most of the other contactees I have met or heard lecture sound patently fraudulent or are obviously seriously unbalanced. Sometimes going to hear a contactee talk reminds me of that horrible pastime of years gone by —going down to the mental institution to watch the antics of the people confined there. There is none of this in Betty Hill. My impression was that she is an eminently sane, practical, and cheerful woman who tells her story in a completely straightforward manner.

I found that there was a distinct air of a rehearsed performance when she recounted her experience. It could hardly be otherwise, however—over the last ten years she must have repeated the story thousands of times, under a variety of conditions. And for whatever it is worth, I would venture the opinion that Betty Hill is telling what she believes to be the truth.

But must we accept it as the truth? As I mentioned, there

is no confirming evidence that the described events, or anything like them, took place. What about the "star map"? Is it possible that Betty Hill, a woman with no background in astronomy, could have drawn a map that perfectly matches the placement of a certain group of stars? Well, perhaps, but the trouble is that her "star map" *doesn't* exactly match the arrangement of any known group of stars, not without some fudging, ignoring one feature and emphasizing another. This was pointed out in detail by astronomers Steven Soter and Carl Sagan and by UFO critic Robert Scheaffer. Scheaffer noted that there have already been at least three different "identifications" of Betty Hill's stars.

Writing in *Official UFO,* Scheaffer has said:

> There are simply too many patterns that fit Betty Hill's sketch. Random star positions, when rotated, sorted, and manipulated, can be made to match nearly any preestablished pattern, as long as we are willing to expend enough time and effort to obtain a match.

The evidence of the "star map," which seemed so impressive in the television dramatization of *The Interrupted Journey,* does not hold up very well in real life.

One of the reasons this particular case became so famous is that the Hills' story came out only under hypnosis. There is a general impression that a hypnotized person *must* tell the truth. This is nonsense. A hypnotized person may tell what he or she *believes* to be the truth, but there is no guarantee that this belief will not turn out to be a fantasy.

Most people who have a passing familiarity with the Hill case are under the impression that Dr. Simon, the psychiatrist, endorses the Hills' story as being objectively true. This, however, is not how Dr. Simon feels at all. One has to read *The Interrupted Journey* rather carefully to discover this, but buried way down in Chapter 12 is the information that Dr. Simon himself believes that the abduction story is a shared fantasy. This point was hardly brought out at all in the TV movie.

Well, then, if Betty and Barney Hill were not abducted by the occupants of a UFO, what happened to them during their "lost hours"? More to the point—were there, in fact, any lost hours? Scheaffer has pointed out that the time of the alleged encounter with the UFO has never been clearly established. Barney Hill, it seems, spent a good deal of time driving very slowly, or just sitting in his parked car watching the light in the sky; afterward he appeared to have no clear idea how long he had spent doing this. So there may be no lost time to account for at all.

What really happened during the drive? There are lots of theories, none provable. It's safest to say that no one knows. But it should be well understood that the case for an abduction by extraterrestrials is not nearly as strong as UFO buffs would like us to believe.

Rivaling the Hill case in publicity was the alleged abduction of two men in Pascagoula, Mississippi. The two men, Charles Hickson and Calvin Parker, said they were fishing on an abandoned pier on the night of October 11, 1973. Then, according to their story, they saw a brightly lighted object descend to the ground near them and three rather weird-looking creatures get out. The creatures were about five feet tall and covered with grayish, wrinkled skin; each had protuberances where nose and ears should be. The creatures took the men aboard their craft and subjected them to the sort of physical examination that the Hills were supposed to have undergone.

In the Hill case, the subjects were at first reluctant to discuss their experiences; but the Pascagoula incident became famous at once because Hickson was not merely willing but extremely anxious to talk about what had happened. Indeed, he sought to capitalize on it. Parker, the younger of the two men, claimed to have passed out when the creatures grabbed him, and he never said too much.

A number of investigators, including Dr. Hynek, said that as far as they could tell the two men were relating the truth as they understood it. Unfortunately for the two men, on television talk shows they did not come across as looking particularly trustworthy, and the fame of the case faded rather quickly.

Naturally, skeptic Phil Klass assumed from the beginning that the story was false. He dug up the fact that at the time of the incident Hickson had been recently fired from his previous job for "unsuitable" conduct, and that while he was employed again at the time of the incident he was badly in need of money and clearly hoped to make some selling his story. Hickson tried to contact a local newspaper even before he contacted the sheriff to talk about his "abduction."

Klass also found a bridge tender who had been on duty at a spot near the pier where the abduction was supposed to have taken place. He should have seen a brightly lighted spaceship land, but he didn't.

One of Hickson's primary claims to truthfulness was that he had taken and passed a lie-detector test. Now, a lie detector, or polygraph, is not infallible. But if properly administered by qualified operators, a lie-detector test is reasonably accurate.

The dogged Klass found some oddities in Hickson's test. It seems that Hickson, on the advice of a lawyer he had hired, had gone all the way to New Orleans to find a polygraph operator to his liking. There were qualified operators much closer at hand. The New Orleans operator himself, while trained, was not certified, and was far from being the most experienced polygraph operator available. Klass offered to pay for another lie-detector test for Hickson, but Hickson declined. Hickson also declined to take a lie-detector test at a 1975 UFO conference, after having first agreed to take the test.

None of Klass's evidence proves conclusively that the Pascagoula incident was a hoax. On the other hand, it doesn't leave you with a great feeling of confidence that it wasn't, either.

The Travis Walton case is even worse. It would not be worth discussing at all except that it reveals that some of those who have hotly charged a "cover-up" of the truth about UFOs are not above doing a little covering up themselves.

Walton was one of a group of seven young woodcutters who were working in the Apache–Sitgreaves National Forest in Arizona. On November 5, 1975, they were driving to work when they saw a UFO hovering nearby. Walton jumped out of the car and ran toward the UFO, but was "zapped" by a glowing beam from the craft. The rest of the group drove off in a panic, and when they returned to the spot they found that Walton had disappeared.

The six young men took lie-detector tests on November 10. Five passed, and the test for the sixth was inconclusive. Five days after he had disappeared, Travis Walton showed up again; he was in a very confused mental state, insisting he could remember nothing of what had happened.

Phil Klass went after the Walton case too, and turned up one startling and utterly damning fact. Walton took a lie-detector test on November 14, 1975, just four days after his "return." The test was given by an experienced polygraph operator, paid for by the tabloid *National Enquirer,* and arranged by Jim Lorenzen, director of the Aerial Phenomena Research Organization. Walton flunked the test cold. But neither the readers of the *Enquirer* nor the members of APRO were informed of this fact. The *Enquirer,* which owned the test results, chose to keep them secret.

Months later, Walton did pass a lie-detector test given by a far less experienced operator. When Klass contacted the head of the polygraph organization for which this second operator worked and reviewed the details of how the test had been conducted, the man agreed, "This test should be invalidated."

As for the tests of the other six men, what Klass found was that the questions they were asked related only to the possibility that a crime had been committed. There was only one question about the UFO itself, and the man who administered the tests admitted to Klass, "That one question does not make it a valid test for verifying the UFO incident."

There is more, but it is all rather dreary.

Naturally, a lot of UFO buffs don't like Phil Klass very much. They have tried to brush aside the objections he raises with the phrase "Klass dismissed." But as these examples have demonstrated, he has found things that other UFO investigators, had they been committed to finding the truth, rather than to merely furthering their own theories, should have found themselves.

Klass cannot be dismissed as easily as all that.

I must add, however, that some of the UFO organizations, including NICAP, had grave doubts about the Walton case from the start. The official NICAP newsletter printed a full report of Klass's findings. NICAP has feuded off and on with APRO for many years, so the Klass exposé gave it a double bonus—a chance to serve the truth and to stick it to an old rival.

This 1950 photo shows a saucerlike object flying over a farm in McMinnville, Oregon.

A UFO photographed by highway inspector Rex Heflin in Santa Ana, California, in 1965.

UNITED PRESS INTERNATIONAL PHOTO

Ralph Ditter of Zanesville, Ohio, an amateur astronomer and photographer, took this picture of what he described as an object from another solar system in 1967.

Saucerlike objects observed over Marseilles, France, are in fact unusual cloud formations.

U.S. NAVY PHOTO FROM UNITED PRESS INTERNATIONAL

Ray Palmer, the original flying-saucer enthusiast—the man who got Ufology off the ground.

JIM OBERG

Donald E. Keyhoe (right), who devoted years to publicizing his theory that information about UFOs was being suppressed by an Air Force cover-up, is shown here with Ufologist Richard Hall.

GEORGE W. EARLEY

Phil Klass, arch-UFO skeptic.

GEORGE W. EARLEY

Dr. J. Allen Hynek (right), the most famous American UFO investigator, and Dr. James Hardler were photographed during the investigation of the Pascagoula "kidnapping" case.

Erich von Däniken claimed that the Nazca lines (left) were drawn by ancient Peruvians to guide voyagers from outer space.

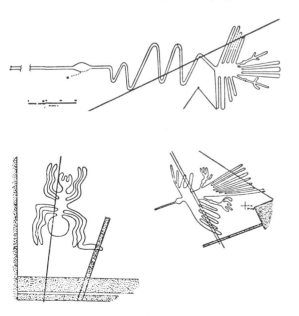

U.S. AIR FORCE TECHNICAL INFORMATION

This questionnaire has been prepared so that you can give the U.S. Air Force as much information as possible concerning the unidentified aerial phenomenon that you have observed. Please try to answer as many questions as you possibly can. The information that you give will be used for research purposes. Your name will not be used in connection with any statements, conclusions, or publications without your permission. We request this personal information so that if it is deemed necessary, we may contact you for further details.

1. When did you see the object?

Day	Month	Year

2. Time of day: _____ Hours _____ Minutes

(Circle One): A.M. or P.M.

3. Time Zone: (Circle One): a. Eastern   b. Central   c. Mountain   d. Pacific   e. Other _____

(Circle One): a. Daylight Saving   b. Standard

4. Where were you when you saw the object?

Nearest Postal Address _____   City or Town _____   State or County _____

5. How long was object in sight? (Total Duration) _____ Hours _____ Minutes _____ Seconds

a. Certain   b. Fairly certain   c. Not very sure   d. Just a guess

5.1 How was time in sight determined? _____

5.2 Was object in sight continuously?   Yes _____   No _____

6. What was the condition of the sky?

DAY   a. Bright   b. Cloudy

NIGHT   a. Bright   b. Cloudy

7. IF you saw the object during DAYLIGHT, where was the SUN located as you looked at the object?

(Circle One) a. In front of you   b. In back of you   c. To your right   d. To your left   e. Overhead   f. Don't remember

FORM
FTD OCT 62 164   This form supersedes FTD 164 Jul 61 which is obsolete.

8. If you saw the object at NIGHT, what did you notice concerning the STARS and MOON?

8.1 STARS (Circle One):
a. None
b. A few
c. Many
d. Don't remember

8.2 MOON (Circle One):
a. Bright moonlight
b. Dull moonlight
c. No moonlight—pitch dark
d. Don't remember

9. What were the weather conditions at the time you saw the object?

CLOUDS (Circle One):
a. Clear sky
b. Hazy
c. Scattered clouds
d. Thick or heavy clouds

WEATHER (Circle One):
a. Dry
b. Fog, mist, or light rain
c. Moderate or heavy rain
d. Snow
e. Don't remember

10. The object appeared: (Circle One):

a. Solid
b. Transparent
c. Vapor
d. As a light
e. Don't remember

11. If it appeared as a light, was it brighter than the brightest stars? (Circle One):

a. Brighter
b. Dimmer
c. About the same
d. Don't know

11.1 Compare brightness to some common object: _____

12. The edges of the object were:

(Circle One): a. Fuzzy or blurred
b. Like a bright star
c. Sharply outlined
d. Don't remember
e. Other _____

13. Did the object: (Circle One for each question)

a. Appear to stand still at any time?	Yes	No	Don't know
b. Suddenly speed up and rush away at any time?	Yes	No	Don't know
c. Break up into parts or explode?	Yes	No	Don't know
d. Give off smoke?	Yes	No	Don't know
e. Change brightness?	Yes	No	Don't know
f. Change shape?	Yes	No	Don't know
g. Flash or flicker?	Yes	No	Don't know
h. Disappear and reappear?	Yes	No	Don't know

The opening pages of a questionnaire distributed by the Air Force during its investigation of UFO sightings.

When public interest runs high, UFO-watching becomes a popular pastime. Above, watchers in Michigan scan the skies after numerous sightings in 1966; below, a crowd awaits a landing in a scene from the film *Close Encounters of the Third Kind* (1977).

Chapter 11
MONSTERS

GEORGE ADAMSKI AND MOST of the other contactees described their space people as conforming to an Anglo-Saxon ideal of beauty—fair-skinned, golden-haired, clean-featured, slim. In the Pascagoula case, however, the things that were supposed to have grabbed Hickson and Parker were downright ugly— and even worse-looking things have been reported stepping out of UFOs.

For some reason, West Virginia seems to be infested with UFO monsters. Probably there aren't really any more monsters there than there are anywhere else, but the West Virginia monster cases are given the most publicity. Gray Barker, a well-known saucer researcher and prolific writer, lives in Clarksburg, West Virginia, and writes up all of the sightings around there; and John Keel, who has written a number of books on UFO monsters, has spent a lot of time in West Virginia. At any rate, West Virginia bids fair to be the UFO monster capital of the nation, if not of the world.

The first of the big-time West Virginia monsters was seen in that vintage UFO year, 1952. On September 12, two boys from the small town of Flatwoods, West Virginia, claimed that they had seen some sort of craft land or crash over the crest of a hill behind their house. The boys, a couple of friends, and one adult went up the hill to take a look.

What they found, according to one of the witnesses, was "a fire-breathing monster ten feet tall, with a bright green body and a blood red face" that waddled toward them with "a bouncing, floating motion." The witness added, "It looked worse than Frankenstein. It couldn't have been human."

The little group beat it down the hill fast and called the sheriff's office. The sheriff didn't think much of the story, but a party went up the hill to investigate anyway. They expected to find nothing, and found nothing.

The Air Force was contacted too. It didn't think much of the story either. An Air Force investigator was quoted as commenting, "If he walks, he's an Army problem. Let us know when he flies."

While the press didn't take the "Flatwoods monster" seriously, they did take it. The story got quite a bit of publicity, and two of those who said they'd seen the monster came to New York and were interviewed on several radio shows.

Serious investigators think that the Flatwoods monster, if it wasn't a hoax, was probably the result of fear and heightened imagination. UFOs were a hot topic in 1952; everyone was aware of them. As the group trudged up the hill they must have become more and more excited and frightened. At the top of the hill they saw two bright eyes peering at them from about ten feet off the ground. What they saw was most probably eyeshine from a possum or other animal sitting in a tree, but in the tense and emotional atmosphere of the moment the eyes became those of a monster. Imagination, and perhaps a desire for attention, did the rest.

Within a relatively short time those involved in the incident wouldn't talk about it anymore. But accounts of the Flatwoods monster still appear regularly in books by the more enthusiastic and unrestrained of the Ufologists.

The next West Virginia monster biggie was "Mothman." Mothman was a winged something-or-other that began appearing in and around Point Pleasant, West Virginia, in November of 1966 (the year, incidentally, of the biggest UFO flap since 1952). The thing was first spotted by some teenagers who had been driving around a deserted arsenal known as the TNT area. They saw something about six feet tall and gray standing alongside the road. When they got close to it it spread its wings, which reached about ten feet from tip to tip, and rose straight up in the air. That scared the teenagers badly, and they beat it back to town. They said the car hit one hundred miles an hour on the return trip, but the winged thing was able to keep pace with them. Finally it seemed to tire of the chase, veered off in another direction, and disappeared.

The teenagers were not at all shy about telling others what they had seen. They even held a press conference the next morning, and the tale was picked up by the wire services. Most accounts treated it in only a semiserious manner, and the story looked like a short-lived sensation.

Then other people began reporting that they had seen the "thing" too. John Keel, who spent a lot of time in West Virginia investigating the Mothman case, wrote:

> Everyone was now seeing Mothman or the "Bird," or so it seemed. Sightings were reported in Mason, Lincoln, Logan, Kanawha, and Nicholas counties. People were traveling for hundreds of miles to sit in the cold TNT area all night, hoping to glimpse the creature. Those who were unlucky enough to see it vowed they never wanted to see it again. It evoked unspeakable terrors. Like flying saucers, it delighted in chasing cars . . . a very unbirdlike habit. . . .

Suggestions about what Mothman might be began to pop up. One theory was that it was a sandhill crane or some other large but quite ordinary bird that had wandered into the area. The wardens of a nearby wildlife refuge, however, disputed that idea, saying that no unusual large birds had been observed.

Another suggestion was that the tale had begun as a hoax and had spread through the operation of our old friend "mass hysteria" and the sensationalizing efforts of people like John Keel. Believers in Mothman haughtily brushed aside all such inferences.

The notion that seemed to catch on was that Mothman had

come from a UFO. Now, the connection between Mothman and UFOs is a tenuous one. Some people said that UFOs had been spotted in the area before, during, and after the appearances of Mothman. But an actual UFO sighting wasn't really necessary, because there was a general tendency to connect all strange and unusual events with the actions of UFOs.

On December 15, 1967—more than a year after Mothman had first been sighted—the Silver Bridge, which spanned the Ohio River near Point Pleasant, suddenly collapsed. It was an awful tragedy in which many were killed. Somehow or another those who were involved in the doings of Mothman ascribed the disaster to the appearance of the creature. In any event, reported sightings of Mothman dropped off sharply after the collapse of the bridge.

Vegetable Man was another monster from the same area. Jennings Fredericks, who lived near Fairmont, West Virginia, said that he was walking through the woods in mid-July of 1968 when he suddenly found that he had become entangled with a bush of some sort. The "bush" turned out to be the flexible arm of a creature that had a body like the stalk of some huge plant. It had a face, of sorts, with slanting eyes, and pointed ears. The eyes seemed to be able to rotate in order to create a hypnotic effect.

The creature penetrated Fredericks' arm with the needle-like tip of one of its "fingers" and withdrew some blood. Telepathically it communicated this message: "You need not fear me. I wish to communicate. I come as a friend. We know of you all. I come in peace. I wish medical assistance. I need your help!"

The "transfusion," if that is what was going on, took only about a minute. Then the creature released Fredericks and departed in great haste, making huge leaps like some sort of unearthly kangaroo. Fredericks kept quiet about the frightening encounter, fearing that no one would believe him, but he finally revealed all in an interview with Gray Barker, who then printed a full report on Vegetable Man (with drawings) in the March, 1976, issue of his newsletter. Once again, there is no direct connection between Vegetable Man and a UFO; the connection is assumed. It seems almost natural.

Until the early spring of 1977 I had never visited West Virginia, the scene of all these, and so many other, exciting UFO events. So when I had an opportunity to give a lecture at Fairmont College, right in the heart of West Virginia's monster country, I was delighted. I figured that I was going to learn more from the audience than they would learn from me. I thought that I would impress them with my knowledge of local affairs (usually lecturers have never even heard of the place where they're lecturing). So I talked of Mothman and the Flatwoods monster, and even mentioned Vegetable Man. No one at Fairmont had ever heard of them! They thought I was putting them on and making up stories. Somebody may have been, but it wasn't me. I was bitterly disappointed.

Of course, West Virginia isn't the only place where people report seeing monstrous creatures that they somehow associate with UFOs. Mrs. Wesley Symmonds of Cincinnati, Ohio, saw four "bug-eyed" creatures along the side of the road while she was driving through Georgia. She said the creatures were bipeds with pointed chins and thin arms that seemed to end in clawlike appendages. They looked very much like the Bug-Eyed Monsters, or BEMs, that were a staple of pulp science fiction for so many years. Back in the '40s hardly a month went by without a magazine like *Thrilling Wonder Stories* appearing with a cover on which one of these BEMs was menacing a semiclad and very shapely girl.

Ted Bloecher, a cataloger of UFO events, says that a person he identifies only as R.H. of Loveland, Ohio, made a strange sighting quite near the place where Mrs. Symmonds saw her "bug-eyed" creatures. The beings R.H. saw were about three feet tall, grayish in color, and had a lopsided appearance. They also had huge lipless mouths that made their faces look rather froglike.

In their book *Encounters with UFO Occupants,* Coral and Jim Lorenzen report the tale of a Mr. S. (Like so many who claim to have seen the occupants of UFOs, Mr. S. insists on anonymity.) The encounter took place in California over the Labor Day weekend of 1964. Mr. S. had been out hunting but had become separated from his companions. He saw a light in the sky that he first assumed was from a rescue helicopter looking for him. He soon discovered, however, that the light was actually coming from a strange, dome-shaped craft that had landed a few hundred yards away. Then he noted that there were three "entities" moving through the brush. Here is the description given by the Lorenzens:

> The two figures at the bottom of the tree seemed to S. to be approximately five feet five inches in height, clothed in silvery gray material with a covering that went up over the head straight from the shoulder. . . .
>
> Shortly after the two figures arrived at the base of the tree S. saw another figure come from the direction of the dome. . . . This third entity was gray, dark gray, or black. It had no discernible neck, but two reddish orange "eyes" glowed and flickered where the "head" would be. It also had an opening where a mouth would be, which, when it opened, seemed to drop open, making a rectangular hole in the face. The mouth extended completely across the "face" area.

Mr. S. had the distinct impression that the third "entity" was a robot.

If one is to believe compilers of UFO lore, an awful lot of people see Bigfoot-like creatures in connection with UFO sightings or landings. There are also a host of small green creatures. (Yes, people do see little green men, but they see a lot of other things too.) Some Ufological theorists have attempted to link all monster sightings—Bigfoot, the Loch Ness monster, sea serpents, vampires, werewolves, the works—with UFOs.

For sheer oddness, however, I believe that the space monsters sighted by a Mr. C.A.V. of Lima, Peru, should stand near the top of anybody's list. Mr. C.A.V. said that in 1957 he came across a saucerlike spaceship near a highway on the outskirts of Lima. Outside the spaceship stood two amoebalike creatures that he described as looking like rough-textured bananas. They were about five feet tall and joined together. The creatures spoke English "as if it came from speakers." Among the things that the outer-space bananas told Mr. C.A.V. was that they were sexless, and they proved the point by dividing right before his eyes.

Chapter 12
SWAMP GAS

WE HAVE SPENT THE LAST FEW CHAPTERS exploring the wilder side of the world of UFOs. It is now time to return to the march of events, to get back to the world as we know it— or as most of us know it, anyway.

We had abandoned the chronological narrative way back in the 1950s, with the Air Force's Project Blue Book trying to hold off what it saw as the forces of confusion and panic through a maladroit mixture of debunking and doing nothing. On the other side, the UFO buffs, now led by Major Donald Keyhoe and his National Investigations Committee for Aerial Phenomena (NICAP was formed in 1956), insisted that the Air Force was really covering up the biggest story in human history. Finally, giving up all hope that the Air Force could ever be made to tell the "truth" about UFOs, NICAP began to press for congressional hearings into the UFO situation.

It was beginning to look as if the Air Force position—"UFOs are nothing to be concerned about and if we stop worrying they will go away"—would prevail through sheer inertia and boredom. After the excitement of 1952, the number of UFO sightings reported to the Air Force began to fall off once again. Then in 1957 there was a sudden and, from the Air Force point of view, alarming rise in the number of reported sightings— there were 1,006 that year. But the next year things quieted down again. In 1963 fewer than four hundred sightings were reported. To some of us it seemed as if UFOs were going to go the way of the dodo bird.

But in 1964 the number of reported sightings was on the rise again. It went up even further in 1965, and in 1966 a whopping 1,060 UFO sightings were officially reported to the Air Force. It was the biggest UFO year since the golden days of 1952 and the "invasion" of Washington, D.C. Not only were a large number of sightings reported, but some of them really managed to capture nationwide attention. (The number of UFO sightings and publicity about UFOs tend to reinforce each other. If many sightings are reported there is more publicity, which in turn stimulates more sightings—or at least more reports.)

If there was one single event that really turned the whole UFO story around in the 1960s, it was what happened on the campus of Hillsdale College in Michigan and in the nearby town of Dexter on the nights of March 20 and 21, 1966.

A relatively unpublicized prelude to these events took place a day earlier near Milan, Michigan, a small town about sixteen miles southeast of Dexter and nine miles south of Ann Arbor, where the University of Michigan has its main campus. In some ways the Milan sighting was the most spectacular of all the Michigan sightings that March, though it was overshadowed and nearly forgotten in the events of the following days.

On March 19, Washtenaw County police sergeant Nuel Schneider and deputy David Fitzpatrick received a report that brightly lighted UFOs were passing over the town of Milan. Schneider later told William B. Mead of United Press International, "We got a call on one that went by and lit the whole city up. We saw about three of them way out. We got closer to Milan, in a cornfield, and started taking pictures. We watched from two in the morning until seven. A top turned upside down is what it looked like to us. We saw lights and we could see something of a form when we got binoculars."

The following night Frank Mannor and his son saw what appeared to be a large glowing object rising from a swamp near the Mannor farmhouse. Mannor called the police at once.

Patrolman Robert Hunawill of Dexter said one glowing object "flew over the top of us" as he and other policemen were driving to the scene. Mannor and his son said they'd gotten within a few hundred yards of the glowing "thing." They said it was about the size of a car, shaped like a football, and pitted. Both the Mannors and the police reported hearing sounds like the echoes of a ricocheting bullet as the object sped off.

The next evening at least sixty-two and perhaps as many as eighty-seven women students at Hillsdale College rushed to their dormitory windows. They were quickly joined by William Van Horn, an undertaker and the county's civil defense director, and their housemother, Mrs. Kelly Hearn, who was also an assistant dean and had once been a newspaper reporter. What this crowd saw was a glowing object hovering over a swampy area a few hundred yards away. According to the witnesses, the object first headed toward the dormitory, then retreated back to the swamp. "It was like a squashed football," said Holly Davis, a freshman from Canfield, Ohio.

These sightings, even with their multiple witnesses, were unexceptional. But UFO excitement was on the rise and the Michigan story was picked up by virtually every newspaper and every radio and TV news program in the country. The Air Force felt that it was under tremendous pressure to explain what the people in Michigan had seen—and to explain it quickly.

So Project Blue Book sent Dr. J. Allen Hynek out to Michigan to investigate. He talked to witnesses and slogged around in the swamps looking for clues. The place was swarming with policemen (some of whom believed that Michigan was being invaded by spaceships), and with reporters who wanted answers.

Exactly what happened next is a matter of some dispute. Hynek has said the Air Force ordered him to hold a press conference. Major Hector Quintanilla, who was head of Project Blue Book at the time, says that Hynek *asked* to hold a news conference because, he said, he could explain the UFOs, and that he was given permission to do so.

Whoever originated the idea, and whether the Air Force ordered it or not, a press conference was held. It was even bigger and more hectic than the press conference on the 1952 Washington sightings. Over one hundred reporters, including TV cameramen, jammed into Detroit's Press Club to listen to and question astronomer J. Allen Hynek. Hynek said the atmosphere was that of a circus, with everyone pressuring him for a single answer to all UFO questions. Hynek concedes that the press conference did not go well.

Hynek told reporters, "A dismal swamp is a most unlikely place for a visit from outer space." He went on to explain how rotting vegetation produces "swamp gas." This gas "can be trapped by ice and winter conditions" and released suddenly when the ground thaws. The gas makes "popping noises."

Hynek did not dogmatically assert that he had the "solution" to the UFO mystery. "I emphasize . . . that I cannot prove in a court of law that this is the full explanation of these sightings. It appears very likely, however, that the combination of the conditions of this particular winter, an unusually mild one in this area, and the particular weather conditions that night— there was little wind in either location—were such as to have produced this unusual and puzzling display."

All the witnesses to the sightings loudly disagreed with Hynek's theory. But far worse, from a public-relations point of view, reporters fastened on the phrase "swamp gas." It sounded appropriately foolish, and it caught the public fancy. Ridicule can be deadly for an idea, and no UFO explanation has ever been as thoroughly ridiculed as Hynek's swamp gas. Within days a flood of hostile press and public reaction poured in. The general consensus seemed to be that the explanation, not the sighting, was "swamp gas."

Yet despite all the ridicule heaped upon it, the swamp-gas theory is a perfectly credible one. Swamp gas, marsh gas, or methane gas has long been believed responsible for the phenomenon known as *ignis fatuus* or will-o-the-wisp—a flickering light often seen over marshy areas. The phenomenon has been known for centuries, and people have often been fooled and terrified by it. But none of this got through the laughter. A lot of people were convinced that Hynek was an Air Force puppet and that he had tried to "whitewash" the entire incident. Hynek's position must have been particularly painful, for by then he was really beginning to believe that UFOs were important.

Hynek also stated that the photographs taken by the policemen of the UFOs sighted near Milan on March 19 were in fact photographs of the moon and the planet Venus. This explanation was never widely challenged, but it never became widely known, either. All that most people ever heard about was the swamp gas.

In May, 1966, the Gallup Poll surveyed the American public on the subject of UFOs. Gallup found that 96 percent of the people had either heard or read something about the subject. Ninety-six percent was one of the highest recognition figures Gallup had ever found on any subject. At that time, 46 percent of those who had heard of UFOs thought they were "real," while 29 percent said they were imaginary. The percentage of Americans who believe UFOs are "real" has continued to rise; the last Gallup survey on the subject, taken in 1973, found that it stood at 51 percent. The 1966 Gallup survey also found that of those who had heard of UFOs, some 5 percent thought they had actually seen one. In 1973 that figure was 11 percent. If the surveys were accurate reflections of American attitudes, it means that some nine million people had seen a UFO by 1966, and over twenty million had seen one by 1973.

What came to be known as the "incident at Exeter" first got wide public coverage in 1966, though it had taken place the year before. In the early morning of September 3, 1965, eighteen-year-old Norman Muscarello was hitchhiking back to his home in Exeter, New Hampshire, when he saw a brilliantly glowing object coming toward him across an open field. The terrified Muscarello jumped into a ditch and watched the object drift by and circle a nearby house. He described it as being about eighty feet wide and having red, pulsating lights.

Muscarello managed to flag down a car and get to the Exeter police station, where he told his story. Reginald Toland, who was on desk duty, was inclined to think there might be something to the story, because a short while earlier a woman had reported that her car had been followed for miles by a silent object with flashing red lights. This had supposedly happened in the same area where Muscarello had made his sighting.

Toland directed patrolman Eugene Bertrand to go back to the sighting location with Muscarello and check it out. When the pair first arrived at the scene everything looked normal, and Bertrand was convinced that the hitchhiker had seen a helicopter or some other conventional object. Then suddenly Muscarello screamed, "I see it! I see it!"

A huge, roundish, glowing object rose slowly from behind the trees, and both men ran back toward the patrol car. Just then another policeman arrived on the scene, and he also saw the object.

The incident received some local publicity but did not catch the public fancy, and would have been forgotten if it had not come to the attention of John Fuller, a columnist for the respected magazine *Saturday Review*. Fuller, who said he was a skeptic, was looking around for a UFO case to investigate for his column. NICAP suggested the Exeter sighting. So Fuller went up to Exeter and began asking questions.

Fuller was impressed by the intelligence and apparent honesty of the witnesses, and he found a lot more people who had made sightings too. He wrote all this up for the *Saturday Review*, and later expanded his article into a book called *Incident at Exeter*. Before the book was published in 1966, extracts from it were printed in *Look* magazine, which had a very large circulation. This insured a wide readership for the book.

What made *Incident at Exeter* different from all the UFO books that had come before was that Fuller was not only a respected writer, he was a good one. Donald Keyhoe always wrote as though he were shouting at the top of his lungs. Besides, he often sensationalized and fictionalized his facts. Other writers, like Frank Scully, were patently untrustworthy. John Fuller brought an air of respectability to the subject of UFOs.

I remember a small incident with John Fuller that illustrates how emotional the subject of UFOs did (and still can) become. I had written a critical but not unfriendly review of *Incident at Exeter*. Fuller had acknowledged that the review was "very fair" and much better than he had received from many others. We had both been invited to discuss UFOs on educational television. The show was to be ultrarespectable, because it was to be taped and shown in schools. We were supposed to be two gentlemen discussing a controversial topic in a polite fashion. That's what I wanted, and I'm sure that's what Fuller wanted too. But no sooner had we begun taping than we found ourselves embroiled in a red-faced shouting match. I don't know what happened. As I recall it, Fuller lost his temper first. His recollection (if he still remembers the incident at all) is probably just the opposite.

Whoever started the argument, neither of us could end it when the show ended. It continued out in the hall and in a taxi we shared back to midtown Manhattan. Fuller got out first, and after he did the puzzled taxi driver turned to me and said, "What were you guys yellin' about?"

UFOs had hooked Fuller more deeply than he knew at the

time. He went on to write *The Interrupted Journey*, the story of Betty and Barney Hill, and several other UFO books and articles. More recently he has branched out into psychic subjects. He also left *Saturday Review*, reputedly after a dispute with John Lear, the publication's science editor, who was strongly anti-UFO.

It was *Incident at Exeter* that pulled Phil Klass into the world of UFOs. He read the book and decided he had a good idea that what the people of that New Hampshire town had seen were plasmas—masses of luminous, ionized air particles. (A plasma is a form of ball lightning.) Klass thought the plasma theory could explain many other UFO sightings too. He wrote an article that said so, and got so much comment, mostly hostile, that he felt he could not abandon the fight. "In the language of drug addiction, and I fear there is some similarity, I was hooked."

For some time Donald Keyhoe and NICAP had been clamoring for congressional hearings on the Air Force's "cover-up" of the truth about UFOs. In 1966 Gerald Ford, who was then a congressman from Michigan and the House minority leader, was getting a lot of letters from back home expressing dissatisfaction with Air Force procedures—and a real concern about UFOs. He strongly recommended that a congressional committee investigate the subject.

The House Armed Services Committee picked up Ford's suggestion, and on April 5, 1966, it began the first congressional hearings on UFOs. The hearings were brief and undramatic. Hynek read what he called a "daring" statement in which he, for the first time, came out of the closet with his objections to the way the Air Force had conducted the UFO investigations, and gave recommendations for an expanded scientific examination of the subject. Hynek had been badly stung by the ridicule of "swamp gas."

Secretary of the Air Force Harold Brown said that he was considering setting up a scientific panel to do an independent investigation of UFOs. The House committee members greeted this statement with unconcealed joy. An independent scientific panel would get everybody off the hook. Instantly the scientific panel, which had been just a thought before the hearings began, became an absolute necessity.

So, with a few UFO jokes, the committee closed the hearing, and the search for a suitable scientific panel began. It was not to be an easy one.

Chapter 13
THE CONDON COMMITTEE

ANYBODY WHO KNOWS ANYTHING about university funding would figure that a government grant of $300,000 to study anything would be pretty easy to get rid of. Grantsmanship— that is, getting large sums of money to study some subject—is one of the necessary skills of modern academic life.

Yet when the Air Force started looking around for a leading university to take its $300,000 (later the figure rose to $500,000) to study UFOs, there were no immediate takers. Reportedly institutions like Harvard, MIT, and the University of California turned the project down because they just didn't want to get involved with UFOs. Events were later to show how wise their caution had been.

The Air Force also tried to interest the National Center for Atmospheric Research in Boulder, Colorado. The Center wouldn't take the money either, but did suggest the University of Colorado, which finally accepted the job.

A scientist of stature was needed to head the project, and the obvious choice seemed to be Colorado's Dr. Edward U. Condon. Condon was a physicist with an international reputation. As former head of the National Bureau of Standards, he had administrative as well as scientific experience. And he had another outstanding qualification: he had a reputation for courage in resisting government pressure.

Back in the 1950s there was a lot of anti-Communist hysteria in the United States. Many scientists and other intellectuals were accused of being Communists or Communist sympathizers. By and large the charges were not true. But many people lost their jobs or had their reputations ruined anyway.

One of the chief Communist-hunters of those days was an
ambitious young politician from California named Richard
Nixon. Nixon had parlayed his reputation for exposing "Communists" into a seat in the U.S. House of Representatives and
then a seat in the U.S. Senate. (He acquired a national reputation and became Vice-President under Dwight D. Eisenhower
in 1952.) One of Nixon's special targets was Dr. Edward U.
Condon, whom Nixon accused of being a "security risk." Nixon
often boasted that he was responsible for having Condon's
security clearance lifted.

But Condon refused to give up. He brought his case before
a variety of loyalty review boards. It was a long, difficult, and
dirty fight, but ultimately Condon emerged victorious. His
scientific and political reputation was unstained. Very few in
his position were able to claim such a victory. Though Condon
probably didn't know it at the time, he was going to need all
his courage in the upcoming UFO fight.

At first, Condon (like any sane man) didn't want the job. He
had had no previous interest in UFOs. But he was finally flat-
tered and cajoled into heading the study group—somebody
had to do it, he was told.

Condon's appointment was announced on October 7, 1966,
and there were public expressions of joy and relief. Hynek said
he felt vindicated, and Keyhoe was delighted. But from the
very beginning, there were rumblings of discontent about the
Condon Committee.

I attended the New York press conference at which Dr.
Condon's appointment was announced. Over the next few
days I talked to some of my acquaintances in the Ufological
community. Most of them said that the work of the committee
was doomed to failure. Admittedly, much of this gloomy information was coming from contactees, who were getting it telepathically from the space people. But the predictions turned
out to be far more accurate than most issued by contactees.

In an attempt to avoid controversy, Hynek was not appointed to the committee because he already had a publicly stated position on the subject. Neither was Donald Menzel, the astronomer who had emerged as a fierce foe of UFO buffs in the late 1950s. (In Menzel's view, most UFO sightings could be traced to unusual atmospheric phenomena—or fraud.)

There was to be an appearance of "objectivity" about the committee. In practice, however, an "objective" view is usually one that you already agree with. Condon had not been particularly interested in UFOs before his appointment. He had little faith in the extraterrestrial hypothesis, and made no bones about that.

Though the regular staff members of the Condon Committee had not expressed their opinions about UFOs publicly before they were appointed, there is little doubt that as human beings they did have opinions. Those who were "anti-UFO"— that is, those who believed that the UFO excitement was the result of hoaxes and misinterpretations of natural events— seem to have outnumbered the "pro-UFO" members of the committee—those who believed that there was something extraordinary, and probably extraterrestrial, about UFOs. With both points of view represented, and given the passions that the subject of UFOs inspired, a clash was inevitable.

Within a few months after the study began, the pro-UFO people became disturbed over what they regarded as Condon's negative, even unserious attitude toward the subject. The major battle finally erupted over what came to be known as "the infamous Low memorandum." Robert Low, the project coordinator, had quickly emerged as the leader of the "anti-UFO" faction of the committee. Dr. David Saunders, a Ph.D. psychologist, was head of the "pro-UFO" faction.

In August, 1966, while the University of Colorado was still considering whether to take on the UFO project, Low wrote a memorandum stating what he thought would be the use and final result of such a study. Low expressed the opinion that UFOs were probably not one particular thing and certainly were not extraterrestrial spaceships. Low also said that it would be practically impossible to prove the nonexistence of extraterrestrial spaceships because you couldn't prove a negative proposition, but that an impressive amount of information could be collected that would support the view that people were not really seeing spaceships. There would be a public-relations problem with the scientific community, however, Low pointed out. And in his most famous sentence Low wrote, "The trick would be to describe the project so that, to the public, it would appear a totally objective study, but, to the scientific community, would present the image of a group of nonbelievers trying their best to be objective but having an almost zero expectation of finding a saucer." In short, Low thought it would be important to tip off other scientists to the fact that the committee wasn't made up of saucer-chasing nuts. Low thought that the best way to accomplish this end would be to stress "the psychology and sociology of persons and groups who report seeing UFOs."

It is impossible to say how influential this memorandum was. Condon himself didn't see it. It just got stuck away in a file and forgotten until July, 1967, when one of the committee staff members, Roy Craig, ran across it by accident. Craig showed it to another staff member, Norman Levine, who showed it to David Saunders.

Saunders took the crucial step of going outside the committee itself and showing the memorandum to Keyhoe. Keyhoe told Dr. James E. McDonald, the atmospheric physicist who by that time had eclipsed Keyhoe as the public leader of UFO enthusiasts. Later McDonald got a copy of the memorandum.

Condon and Low remained in blissful ignorance of all this excitement for almost eight months. Then in February, 1968, Low got a long letter from McDonald complaining about the way the project was being handled. Low's memorandum was mentioned, although just briefly. That tore it. Low was enraged. So was Condon. He promptly fired Saunders and Levine and accused them of stealing the memorandum from Low's personal file and releasing it to McDonald. Next Condon's assistant, Mary Lou Armstrong, resigned in protest over the firings.

The fight between the pro- and anti-UFO factions on the committee that had been simmering under the surface for months was now out in the open. John Fuller, who had become fully committed both personally and professionally to UFOs, wrote an article for *Look* magazine entitled "Flying Saucer Fiasco." The article presented the controversy within the committee pretty much from the pro-UFO (and increasingly anti-Condon) side. The thrust of the article was that the Condon Committee could never find extraterrestrial spaceships because it was committed to not finding them.

The Fuller article got wide publicity, and Condon was on the spot. His reaction was to become grumpy and short-tempered. He and Saunders traded threats of libel suits, though in the end nobody sued.

Science, the official publication of the American Association for the Advancement of Science (AAAS), also planned to run an article on the controversy. Condon first agreed to cooperate in the preparation of the article but then changed his mind. He retreated into the position that he was to adopt until the end of the controversy—that it was inappropriate to say anything until the committee's full report was published. The editor of *Science* criticized him for backing out on his commitment to help with the article, and Condon promptly resigned from the AAAS.

The general public, which held the idea that scientific controversy was always a polite and scholarly affair and that all scientific questions could be solved by "an objective study of the facts," was both entertained and confused by this kicking, eye-gouging street fight among Ph.D.s. What the public didn't know is that an awful lot of scientific controversy is conducted at a very high level of bitterness and anger. The fight among the members of the Condon Committee was a bit more public than most scientific disputes, and perhaps a bit nastier. But as scientific disputes go, it was far from unique. Scientists, like ordinary folk, have tempers. Generally nonscientists are not interested in scientific disputes, so they never hear about the everyday name-calling and back-stabbing. They were interested in UFOs, so the controversy got a lot of publicity.

Eventually Congress got back into the act. Congressman Edward Roush of Indiana read the Fuller article in *Look* and said in a speech that "it raised grave doubts as to the scientific profundity and objectivity of the project." At James McDonald's suggestion, Congressman Roush began a new series of congressional hearings on UFOs.

These hearings were sponsored by the House Science and Astronautics Committee. A number of scientists and others who had been allied to the UFO field either testified in person or submitted papers. The committee had one rule: the Condon Committee could not be criticized, because the Condon Committee was an Air Force project, and the proper place to criticize an Air Force project was in the House Armed Services Committee. (Congressmen are notoriously jealous of their territory.) Those invited to testify at the hearings were mostly from the pro-UFO side, and Donald Menzel objected to the panel of witnesses that had been called. But he submitted a paper of his own anyway.

Both Hynek and McDonald, while refraining from open criticism of the Condon Committee, called for further and more extensive study of UFOs, perhaps on a global basis. One hardly had to read between the lines to find criticism of the work of the Condon Committee in such statements.

The House hearings came to an end in July, 1968, just at a moment when it seemed that the furor over UFOs had reached its most frenzied pitch. Then something quite unexpected happened—or, to be more accurate, *nothing* happened. The public lost interest in UFOs. The number of reported sightings began to drop off. Membership in organizations like NICAP declined. The papers stopped printing stories about UFOs and the controversies surrounding them. Except for the dedicated few, people became bored with the subject.

Dr. David Saunders and R. Roger Harkins, a reporter for the Boulder, Colorado, newspaper, published a book called *UFOs —Yes!* late in 1968. It was Saunders' version of his dispute with the Condon Committee and his justification for what he had done. The book was also an attempt to discount, in advance, the expected negative findings by the Condon Committee. John Fuller wrote the introduction to the book.

In line with his new policy of making no more public statements, Condon did not comment on *UFOs—Yes!* And even though the public seemed to have become thoroughly fed up with UFOs, the work of the Condon Committee went forward toward its inevitable conclusion.

Chapter 14
THE END OF AN ERA

CONDON WAS DUE TO TURN HIS REPORT over to the National Academy of Sciences for review before it was made public. (There was, by the way, nothing sinister about this. Review of findings by one's peers before a public announcement is a common scientific procedure.) There was a rumor that the final report was being rushed because Condon's old enemy Richard Nixon had been elected president in November, 1968. In fact, the report was released to the public in January of 1969, just before Nixon's inauguration.

The final report of the Condon Committee was not a unified document. The bulk of it (and it *was* bulky—nearly fifteen hundred pages) was a collection of papers written by committee staff members and by individuals with whom the committee had contracted because of their special knowledge in fields like meteorology and astronomy. These articles covered a vast range of Ufological subjects: the history of UFOs, and UFOs in history; public opinion on UFOs; the psychology of some people who had sighted UFOs; and so forth.

A grand total of ninety-one UFO cases of different types were analyzed in depth. In slightly better than two-thirds of the cases, the committee felt that it had been able to identify the origin of the UFO. This left one-third of the cases unidentified.

These figures provide an excellent example of how two people with different points of view can look at the same set of facts and arrive at entirely different conclusions. Those who were anti-UFO found a two-out-of-three percentage of identification of these cases extremely high. Only good—that is, hard-to-identify—UFO cases had been chosen for investigation in the first place. Since data in UFO cases, even good ones, is invariably incomplete, 100 percent identification, or anything near that, is quite unrealistic, the anti-UFO people asserted.

The pro-UFO people looked at the one-third of the cases that remained unidentified and said that these cases indicated that there had to be "genuine UFOs." And they were right, of course, in the sense that there were thirty sightings for which no causes could be discovered. But the Condon Committee turned up no evidence that these thirty "genuine UFOs"— that is, *unidentified* flying objects—were in fact extraterrestrial spaceships. And, after all, it is spaceships that we are all really interested in.

If the pro-UFO people had been arguing that UFOs were the result of some form of unknown weather phenomenon, say, they might have been making an extremely important scientific argument. But who would care? A few meteorologists, but certainly not millions of ordinary people. There are plenty of unexplained phenomena in the world; what some people see in the sky is one of these. No one can argue with that. The real argument is over whether these unexplained sightings are caused by extraterrestrial spaceships. Since it is impossible to prove absolutely that they are not, the Condon Committee had to make a judgment about whether there was enough evidence to justify spending more government money to continue investigations. The committee decided there was not.

The National Science Association's review panel, made up of eleven scientists, not only approved the report, but praised it highly. The panel found the report "a creditable effort to apply objectively the relevant techniques of science to the solution of the UFO problem."

When the report was issued to the public, it had a foreword written by *New York Times* science editor Walter Sullivan. Sullivan devoted part of his piece to a defense of Condon's actions. One of the major criticisms that had been brought against Condon was that he didn't have a serious attitude toward UFOs, and that he was too interested in the most obviously foolish activities of some of the contactees. Sullivan explained that Condon was "a garrulous soul who loves to spin a yarn." As far as "the infamous Low memorandum" was concerned, Sullivan pointed out that Condon had not seen it when it was written, and did not agree with it after he read it. Saunders, incidentally, did not dispute Condon's assertion that he knew nothing of the Low memorandum, and says that had he (Saunders) known this, he might have acted differently.

Condon's own conclusions about UFOs were really not very different from those reached by the various official Air Force projects, or by the Robertson Panel many years earlier. Condon's recommendations, however, were considerably harsher. While the other studies had recommended a degree of continued investigation, or at the very least a continued public-relations campaign, Condon advised the government to get out of the UFO business altogether. Nothing useful would be discovered, he said, and further study would be a waste of time and money.

Condon also delivered an angry diatribe against teachers who allowed their students to use class time to study UFOs. He said that teachers "should channel their interests in the direction of serious study of astronomy and meteorology, and in the direction of critical analysis of arguments for fantastic propositions that are being supported by appeals to fallacious reasoning or false data."

Condon also noted that a small number of individuals were making money by giving sensationalized lectures and writing sensationalized books on the subject of UFOs. He felt that these people had been responsible for creating a great deal of the UFO excitement, and that they had done it for personal gain.

Shortly after the report was issued, Condon again began to recount his funny UFO stories (and some of them were pretty funny). But there is little doubt that Condon's brush with the world of UFOs had left him angry and embittered.

The reactions to the Condon Report were pretty much what you would expect. Anti-UFO people praised it; pro-UFO people damned it. Indeed, the pro-UFO groups had pretty well discounted it in advance.

There was very little criticism of the actual research that the committee had done. The committee was not accused of having "covered up" or misstated information. Even the conclusions about causes of specific UFO sightings were not widely or hotly challenged.

What the critics did point to repeatedly was the fact that one-third of the cases studied remained unidentified. James McDonald complained that the findings of the committee did not support Condon's own negative conclusions.

Another sore point for the critics was the group of cases the committee had chosen to investigate. They felt that the committee had not looked at many of the most significant cases. Hynek said that the scientists who had done the investigating were inexperienced in Ufological research and had failed to take into account the widespread and international character of the UFO phenomenon.

A few other scientists echoed the views of McDonald and Hynek. Another group of scientists, probably somewhat larger, praised the Condon Report and condemned Ufology as a pseudoscience. But the scientific community in general didn't react much one way or the other, and it is hard to escape the conclusion that they just didn't think UFOs were worth bothering about.

Press reaction was both extensive and generally favorable; only a few dissenting voices on smaller newspapers were raised to challenge the report. One California columnist dug up Condon's old clash with Nixon and decided that the report was following Moscow's "new line."

And how did the general public react? The general public, it seems, didn't care. One hundred thousand paperback copies of the Condon Report were printed and offered for sale, with considerable fanfare. The book was a dud. Today it is far easier to obtain a copy of one of George Adamski's books than it is to get a copy of the Condon Report. Admittedly, the book did not make light or easy reading. Also admittedly, negative conclusions about UFOs are far less exciting than positive ones. But that does not entirely explain why the Condon Report landed with such a dull thud. The downward slide of interest in UFOs, which had begun in 1968, was continuing. The Condon Report may have accelerated this slide, but it didn't start it, and certainly didn't reverse it. *Time* magazine headlined its article on Condon "Saucers' End," and indeed that looked to be the case. But the end of interest in UFOs had been predicted before, and this prediction ultimately proved to be no more accurate than those of the past.

While everything was quiet, the Air Force got a chance to do something that it had been wanting to do for the longest time—get out of the UFO business. The Condon Report had recommended closing down Project Blue Book, and in March of 1969 the Air Force did exactly that. There were few tears shed at its funeral. The Blue Book files were shipped to Maxwell Air Force Base in Alabama, where anyone who wanted to could go and look at them. Some people did, and found that the files contained no great secrets or revelations.

The only UFO news worthy of reporting for the rest of 1969 was a symposium held by the American Association for the Advancement of Science. The participants included people on both sides of the question, and the symposium was probably the most respectable scientific forum on the subject ever held anywhere.

Aside from that, the UFO business was dead. Small UFO organizations went under while the biggest struggled for bare survival. Keyhoe was ousted from the leadership of NICAP in a coup by younger members. One significant new club, the Midwest UFO Network (MUFON), was born in 1969, but its membership remained small and its influence inconsequential for several years. UFO publications withered. Not only did the daily newspapers stop printing UFO tales, even the sensational tabloids, which would print anything if it sold papers, avoided them.

The year 1969, with the publication of the Condon Report and the closing of Project Blue Book, represented the end of an era—but not by any means the end of UFOs.

Chapter 15
OLD ASTRONAUTS

THROUGHOUT THIS BOOK we have discussed the mysterious rise and fall of public interest in the subject of UFOs. Why did Kenneth Arnold's not particularly spectacular 1947 sighting attract the attention that it did, and really begin the era of UFOs? Why was Dr. J. Allen Hynek's 1966 swamp-gas explanation greeted with such scorn and ridicule that the Air Force was practically forced to agree to an independent investigation of UFOs?

And in the matter of timing, consider the extraordinary luck of a Swiss hotelman named Erich von Däniken. In 1968 von Däniken published a book called *Chariots of the Gods?* It quickly became an international best-seller, and was translated into most of the major languages on earth. The book first appeared in the United States in 1970. In it, von Däniken proposed that some forty thousand years ago or so, spacemen (ancient astronauts, as they are popularly called) visited the Earth and imparted to our primitive ancestors some of their advanced technological knowledge. It was this contact with space people, according to von Däniken, that allowed the human race to advance from savagery to civilization in a relatively short period of time. It was these contacts with ancient astronauts that became part of the religious mythology of mankind.

Von Däniken followed *Chariots of the Gods?* with several other books on the same theme; all were nearly as popular as the first. Erich von Däniken became an international celebrity and a very rich man. His books have also spawned a host of imitators.

Objectively speaking, von Däniken had nothing going for him. He was not a trained archaeologist, astronomer, or anything else, except for the training he had had in hotel management. Not only did every scientist around denounce his works as utter nonsense and point to numerous inexcusable errors of fact; his work was also denounced by most of those involved in unorthodox or "fringe" science, including most leading Ufologists. Religious leaders did not care for von Däniken either, for his theories were outspokenly antireligious.

To top it off, von Däniken's personal reputation wasn't very good. Just after he completed *Chariots of the Gods?* he was thrown into jail in Switzerland for embezzlement and fraud. The fraud had nothing to do with his book, but such a conviction does not help to build confidence in an author's veracity. Particularly unsettling was the fact that at the trial a psychiatrist who had examined von Däniken described him as a prestige-seeker, a liar, and an unstable and criminal psychopath with a hysterical character. This description was given wide publicity. Yet while von Däniken was serving out his year in prison he wrote another book that was also extremely successful.

Von Däniken's books are filled to the brim with mistakes and foolishness. That is a conclusion that anybody who has bothered to honestly check out the statements in any of his books has come to. There is room for honorable men and women to disagree about the subject of UFOs. There is no room for disagreement on the subject of von Däniken's theories. Most of the evidence that he presents is either misinterpreted or just plain wrong.

What is perhaps most surprising about the enormous success of Erich von Däniken is that none of his theories are new—they had been around for years before he put them into his book. The idea that Earth was visited by spacemen in the distant past has been a staple of science fiction for perhaps a century now. One of the best treatments of the theme can be found in Arthur C. Clarke's excellent novel *Childhood's End.*

The ancient-astronaut theory was seriously proposed by that popular collector of odd facts, Charles Fort, a man we have mentioned before (see Chapter 2) in connection with UFOs. Fort's influence was so great that today people who collect odd facts about things like the Loch Ness monster or UFOs often call themselves Forteans. But nothing Fort ever wrote became one tenth—one hundredth—as famous as *Chariots of the Gods?*

Let us consider one or two of von Däniken's more popular ideas. Perhaps the most sensational evidence he presented in support of his theory were the figures and lines found in the Peruvian coastal desert.

For a long time it has been known that some ancient people etched lines into the desert surface. Since it almost never rains in the Peruvian coastal desert, the lines, though comparatively delicate, have never been obliterated. Von Däniken incorrectly claims that archaeologists have identified these lines as "Inca roads." There *is* an Inca road in the area, but it cuts right through the lines, which are obviously older. The Incas, who were great road builders, had no interest in the lines.

In the 1950s, when airplanes began to fly over the desert regularly, it was discovered that some of these lines formed gigantic pictures of fantastic birds, spiders, monkeys, and other, unidentifiable beasts. Straight lines ran for long distances, but seemed to begin and end for no particular reason. The true magnitude of this work could be appreciated only from the air, but the lines and figures were made long before airplanes were invented or even thought of.

Who the creators of the lines and figures were was never much of a mystery. The lines were made by the Nazca people, who lived in the area before the rise of the Inca empire. The Nazcas were conquered by the Incas and ultimately wiped out in the aftermath of the Spanish conquest of Peru. Some of the animal designs etched in the desert match designs on Nazca pottery and fabrics.

There is also no particular mystery about how the figures and lines were made. Their creators formed them by moving the pebbles that cover the desert surface, exposing the lighter soil underneath. The task was not a technically difficult one, but it *was* tedious and time-consuming.

This brings us to the real mystery of the Nazca lines and figures. Why would any ancient people go through all the trouble of making something that could be appreciated only from the air? (Von Däniken mentions other ancient examples of drawings so large they can be fully appreciated only from airplanes, but the Nazca drawings are the most spectacular.)

Von Däniken proposes that the lines and figures were used by spacemen to help them land their ships. Now, why any civilization that had the technology to travel from a distant planet would need such primitive landing markers is beyond me. But it is profitless to speculate on the needs of theoretical ancient astronauts.

Von Däniken was not the first person to whom this idea occurred. Practically from the time the lines and figures were first viewed from the air, there was humorous speculation that the area had served as an ancient airfield. This idea, first put forth as a joke, was picked up quite seriously by some of the wilder of the UFO buffs. I first heard it in 1964, and I'm certain it is older than that. The idea never attracted much attention from the general public back then, but it was widely discussed in Ufological circles. It was unquestionably being talked about well before Erich von Däniken wrote *Chariots of the Gods?* Whether he arrived at this idea by himself, or heard it elsewhere and adopted it, I can't say.

Von Däniken not only claims that the Nazca lines mark an ancient airfield used by spacemen—he claims there are pictures of the spacemen themselves. Not in Peru, but in the Tassili Mountains in northern Africa.

About thirty years ago, some ancient drawings were discovered on the wall of a rocky gorge in the Tassili Mountains, which are in the Sahara Desert. These are now called the Tassili drawings, and some of them feature what look a bit like crude representations of men in spacesuits. Archaeologists say the drawings show men in ceremonial masks; von Däniken says they actually do show men in spacesuits. But again, the idea is not original. The discoverers of the drawings laughingly dubbed the people in them "Martians" because they were "reminiscent of the image we usually form of Martians." That was not a very serious suggestion, but it was picked up very seriously by UFO buffs, and only later by von Däniken.

Indeed, the whole idea that human civilization was developed from contact with some ancient superior race from somewhere else is one of the oldest and most persistent themes in occultism. Spacemen merely replaced the people of Atlantis, or Lemuria, or the other mythical lands so beloved in occult lore.

Yet von Däniken put it all together at the right moment—a moment when millions of people throughout the world were ready and willing to accept the idea of prehistoric contact with extraterrestrials. *Chariots of the Gods?* came out at a time when people had already been thinking about UFOs' being visiting spaceships for many years. If, as the UFO buffs believed, spaceships were visiting Earth today, it was perfectly logical to assume that they had also visited in the distant past.

So, in a very real sense, von Däniken was the beneficiary of two decades of UFO speculation. His ancient-astronaut theories are really a part of the world of UFOs. In turn, the popularity of the ancient-astronaut theories helped to keep public attention focused on the subject of extraterrestrial visitations at a time when more orthodox UFO sightings were at a low ebb (if one can use the word "orthodox" in such a context).

Von Däniken says that many of the gods of the ancients who, according to religious mythology, come from the skies were in reality space people. Bolder souls state flatly that Jesus was a spaceman who came to Earth via flying saucer.

In 1968, the year that *Chariots of the Gods?* first appeared in German, a New York minister by the name of Barry H. Downing published a book called *The Bible and the Flying Saucers.* In this book Downing tried to explain all sorts of Biblical miracles and obscure and difficult Bible passages in terms of Ufological lore.

While von Däniken claims only that the human race got civilization from space, others have claimed that we really are biological descendants of space people. The idea that our ancestors were apelike creatures is still a very hard one for many people to accept.

There are a number of variations on this basic human-race-from-space theme. The simplest is that we are the direct descendants of space colonists, but have forgotten our origins. Somewhat more complex is the theory that we are the result of crossbreeding between space people and some form of higher apes.

Max Flindt and Otto Binder, in their book *Mankind—Child of the Stars,* propose that the human race was the result of genetic experiments conducted by space people on terrestrial apes.

A less flattering theory holds that space people once used Earth as a penal colony or mental institution and that we are the descendants of extraterrestrial criminals or lunatics. This is a convenient way of explaining why the human race so often engages in activities that are evil or crazy.

UFOs have become so much a part of our twentieth-century consciousness that practically every idea, every unknown or unexplained fact of life, can be, and has been, explained in Ufological terms.

You think that perhaps I exaggerate? Well, read on and see if I do.

Chapter 16
MYSTERIES EVERYWHERE

EVEN IN THE WORLD OF UFOLOGY, where the improbable is considered ordinary and the impossible probable, some of the ideas that we are going to be discussing in this chapter are pretty farfetched.

Let us start with the assassination of President John F. Kennedy. A large number of Americans are dissatisfied with the "official" explanation of the presidential assassination—that Lee Harvey Oswald alone was responsible. A lot of people think a conspiracy was involved—and some people think UFOs were somehow part of that conspiracy.

One of those who said that he distrusted the Oswald explanation for the assassination was New Orleans district attorney Jim Garrison. Garrison accused a New Orleans businessman, Clay L. Shaw, of having been involved in a complex and rather foggy assassination plot. As far as any outsider could tell, there was no substance at all to Garrison's charges. Clay Shaw was ultimately acquitted, and Garrison himself was defeated in a reelection bid.

Now, you may be asking what all of this has to do with UFOs. Well, in December, 1968, while Garrison was preparing his case against Shaw, one of those he called to New Orleans to testify before the grand jury was Fred Crisman of Tacoma, Washington. Fred Crisman was one of the two men who said in 1947 that he had seen flying saucers off Maury Island in the state of Washington. That incident, as we saw in Chapter 3, was later found to be a hoax.

Crisman gave his secret testimony in New Orleans in December, 1968, and was never again mentioned by Garrison's office. But the connection (such as it is) was not to be missed by UFO buffs.

The March, 1976, issue of *Gray Barker's Newsletter* carried a letter from the original UFO buff, old Ray Palmer himself:

The Fred Crisman summoned to testify in the Clay Shaw trial [he appeared before the grand jury, not at the trial] was the same Fred Crisman who was involved in the Tacoma–Maury Island affair, and the same Fred Crisman who claimed to have shot his way out of a cave in Burma, receiving a hole the size of a dime in his arm from a "ray gun" wielded (he said) by a dero [detrimental robot]. His exact words to me: "For God's sake drop the Shaver cave stories! You don't know what you are dealing with here!" [In case you don't understand that reference, hold on and I'll explain it shortly.] He is the same Fred Crisman who offered to go into a cave in Texas and bring out some ancient machinery if I would send him $500 expense money.

It was not Clay Shaw who was ruined financially, personally, and physically—it was Jim Garrison who was ruined. He was . . . subjected to IRS audit and finally won the case in court, but at tremendous financial cost—which was the IRS goal in the first place. He was also libeled, framed in a drug ring, and hounded from office, finally losing out in a reelection run.

I have Garrison's letter stating that they were one and the same man. I also have my answer to Garrison, predicting that Crisman could not be subpoenaed, that he was CIA and tremendously powerful.

There is a definite link between flying saucers, the Shaver Mystery, the Kennedys' assassinations, Watergate, and Fred Crisman. There is one common denominator for everything that is happening in the world today. That common denominator is right where Shaver said it was—no matter whether you prefer caverns or the lower astral or another dimension.

The letter was signed RAP, just like all those old editorials in *Amazing Stories* and *Fantastic Adventures*.

Unless you are well versed in the ways of Ufological–conspiratorial thinking, you are probably pretty confused by that letter. But before I move on to explain some of the more arcane references, I might just pick up a couple of other "links" between UFOs and the Kennedy assassination.

One of those whom Garrison named as a conspirator with Clay Shaw was David W. Ferrie. Ferrie could never be brought to trial, for he was already dead by the time the accusations were made. But Ferrie had once roomed with a fellow who called himself Reverend Raymond Broshears, pastor of the Church of God of Holy Orthodox Christians (whatever that is). And Broshears had once written a piece accusing Lyndon Johnson of being responsible for the assassination of John F. Kennedy—and it had appeared in a UFO publication called *Orbit*.

And then there were a whole flock of rumors that UFOs had been seen over Dallas during November, 1963, shortly before the Kennedy assassination.

While such *outré* theories are not widely held, they are discussed in certain parts of the UFO subculture, and the people who discuss them are neither illiterate nor insane. Conspiratorial thinking is addictive. It is also circular thinking. Once one steps inside the circle, all things can be logically explained in terms of "the conspiracy." If a fact is missing or does not fit, it can be put down as part of "the cover-up."

Now let us back up and talk about the Shaver Mystery mentioned in Palmer's letter, for that is certainly one of the wilder tales attached to UFOs. Way back in 1944, before UFOs or flying saucers were even invented, Palmer began to publish Richard S. Shaver's accounts of an underground world inhabited by deros—detrimental robots—that were the cause of most of the world's troubles.

The Shaver stories were first presented as science fiction. But Palmer started to get letters from people who said that they too knew of the underground world, and that the deros were giving them trouble. The Shaver series was then pre-sented *not* as straight fiction, but as the product of Shaver's "racial memory" of Earth's distant past. That is, Shaver claimed he was able to "remember" things that had happened thousands of years before he was born.

The basic theme of the Shaver tales was that long ago Earth had been inhabited by a superrace, but because of catastrophic changes in Earth's atmosphere, this race had been forced to retreat to vast underground caves, where some of them still lived. The underground people had created robots to work for them, but over the centuries the robots had become destruc-tive—they were now the deros that caused so much trouble to people on the surface.

In the 1940s the Shaver Mystery became famous or notori-ous, depending on your point of view, in science-fiction circles. Interest in the Shaver Mystery had begun to die down by the time Palmer began espousing the cause of flying saucers, but he never forgot Shaver's underground world, as his 1976 letter to Gray Barker clearly indicates. (Before Shaver's death he and Palmer had a falling-out, and Shaver accused Palmer of distort-ing his ideas.)

If Ray Palmer wasn't the first man to say that flying saucers were extraterrestrial spaceships, he was certainly one of the first. He was also one of the first to become bored with that idea. By the early 1950s he had apparently convinced himself that the idea that flying saucers came from outer space was absurd. It was much more reasonable, he said, to assume that they came from inside the hollow earth. The earth, according to Palmer, is not round—it is doughnut-shaped, with two enor-mous holes at the poles. The flying saucers come from the earth's interior through these holes.

Now, Palmer didn't invent the hollow-earth theory or the holes-in-the-poles idea. Both have a long and complex history —too long and complex to go into here. The incredible thing is that in this day of earth satellites and cross-polar flights, there is still a flourishing belief in the hollow earth.

Recently I was delivering a lecture on odd subjects in New York City. A woman in the audience asked me about the hollow earth and the holes in the poles. I answered at great length, giving the history of the hollow-earth and polar-hole theories, and explaining that if anything was impossible, the hollow earth certainly was. She thanked me and told me that she was very much relieved to find out that the earth wasn't hollow, but I honestly don't think she believed a word I said. Moreover, when she asked the question, not one person in an audience of about two hundred laughed. And a short while later, I got a call from a reporter from one of the country's leading sensationalist tabloids asking me about the hollow-earth theory.

The current hollow-earth best-seller is a book called, appropriately enough, *The Hollow Earth.* It was written by a Raymond T. Bernard. I have never been able to find out who Bernard is, and have entertained the suspicion that the book was really written by Ray Palmer. It sounds like Palmer, it certainly concentrates on many of Palmer's favorite themes, and it quotes generously from the writings of Ray Palmer.

One of Palmer's favorite ideas was that the great polar explorer Admiral Richard E. Byrd discovered the holes at the poles way back in the 1920s, but that the government has "hushed up" this discovery. Writing in his own *Flying Saucer* magazine, Palmer cited a statement apparently made by Byrd in 1947: "I'd like to see that land beyond the Pole. That area beyond the Pole is the center of the great unknown."

Palmer then went on to say:

> When [Byrd's] plane took off from its Arctic base, it proceeded straight north to the Pole. From that point, it flew on a total of 1,700 miles beyond the Pole, and then retraced its

course to its Arctic base. As progress was made beyond the Pole point, iceless lands and lakes, mountains covered with trees, and even monstrous animals moving through the underbrush were observed and reported via radio by the plane's occupants. . . .

What really happened is that one of the pilots on the Byrd expedition (to the Antarctic, not the Arctic) reported finding ice-free lakes in which the water seemed remarkably warm—for the Antarctic. All the rest was added by Palmer, or perhaps was added even before Palmer heard the story. Nevertheless, Palmer thought this tale was good evidence for a mysterious civilization (one involved with UFOs, of course) there under the pole. Palmer also said flying saucers could get out of the hollow earth in the same way a ghost goes through a door. Is that all clear, now?

The lore of the Men in Black holds that they generally don't bother people who say that flying saucers are spaceships from other planets; where they really hit hard is at people who say that UFOs are earthly craft that presumably come from the polar regions. No evidence other than a few anonymous stories has ever been supplied to back up this contention. It is just one of those things that is whispered about by those Ufological researchers who are "in the know." But during the 1950s, some people thought that "the secret" of UFOs was that they came from underneath the North Pole.

In earlier chapters we noted that many UFO tales concern abductions of one sort or another. It is natural, indeed inevitable, that some of the more unrestrained Ufological researchers would link UFOs with the Bermuda Triangle, that fabled area of the South Atlantic where ships and planes are supposed to disappear mysteriously and regularly.

The most famous and most genuinely mysterious of all the Bermuda Triangle disappearances was the one in 1944, when five F–16 fighter bombers on a routine training mission were lost.

The pilots were in radio contact with ground bases until they disappeared. They reported that they had become confused and could not get proper readings from their instruments. The official explanation is that they ran out of fuel and ditched in the stormy ocean at night, and that planes and pilots were lost without a trace. But many doubt this prosaic if tragic explanation, and there are rumors that the squadron leader reported seeing a huge spaceship just before radio contact was lost. Naturally this part of the radio message was said to have been suppressed by the Air Force for fear of causing "panic." Even darker rumors hint that one of the pilots was found alive in a life raft, but that he was totally insane, babbling about weird creatures in a spaceship. He was taken secretly to a mental hospital where, the rumors say, he died without ever regaining his sanity.

One reasonably consistent feature of UFO reports is that the appearance of a UFO causes automobile engines to stall and radios to go dead. UFOs have also frequently been reported in the vicinity of power lines. Skeptic Phil Klass believes that this may be due to the fact that power lines produce glowing plasmas—masses of ionized air. (As we saw in Chapter 12, Klass thinks such plasmas account for many UFO reports.) At any rate, the belief has grown that UFOs draw electrical power from automobiles, power lines, and generating plants. When the northeastern United States and parts of Canada were blacked out in the massive power failure of 1965, the rumor spread that UFOs had been especially numerous in the vicinity of Niagara Falls, where the power failure began, just before all the lights went out. The rumors, however, began after the great blackout, not before, and seemed to be a reflection of what people thought should have happened, not of what actually did happen.

No discussion of UFO mysteries is complete without the

story of the "Philadelphia experiment." In Chapter 8, I mentioned the UFO researcher Morris K. Jessup, who committed
suicide in 1959 under conditions that some UFO buffs found
both mysterious and sinister. Before his death, Jessup wrote a
book called *The Case for the UFO.* After it was published, he
received two letters and a copy of his own book with handwrit-
ten marginal notes from a man who called himself Carlos
Allende or Carl Allen.

Allende said he had either witnessed or heard about (his
letters are not entirely clear) a Navy experiment in which a
ship disappeared briefly from the harbor in Philadelphia and
at the same instant appeared in Norfolk, Virginia. Allende
further stated that many of the crewmen of the ship died, and
others were driven mad, as a result of the experiment. The
mad crewmen, he said, were being kept in a secret, locked
hospital ward. Allende told Jessup that he wondered whether
this method of instantaneous transport had been used by the
Navy to build UFOs.

The Navy not only denied the "Philadelphia experiment"
story, but regarded it as barely worth commenting upon. It is
possible that the whole idea began with experiments in
degaussing—the neutralizing of a ship's magnetism so that it
could pass over magnetic mines without setting them off. A
degaussed ship would, in a sense, disappear—but only mag-
netically; the physical body of the ship would, of course, stay
where it was.

Whatever the origin of the "Philadelphia experiment" idea,
it is quite clear that the Allende letters were crank letters of
the type regularly received by anyone who writes about
unusual subjects. I have gotten a lot of them, some even wilder
than the Allende letters. I throw them away. But Jessup did not
throw away his letters. He showed them to others in the UFO
field, and soon a whole legend grew up around them. The
"Philadelphia experiment" came to be accepted as a fact by
many Ufologists.

Finally, there are "the mysterious cattle mutilations." During the late summer and early fall of 1974, dead cattle with parts of their bodies missing were reported in areas of northeastern Nebraska and eastern South Dakota. This is ranching country, and finding dead cattle on the range is not an uncommon occurrence. It is certainly not ordinarily newsworthy. But reports about the dead and mutilated cattle were printed in local papers. It seemed to many that something strange and sinister was going on. Ranchers were genuinely frightened. They held several meetings and began patrolling the range at night.

Some people believed that the mutilations were the work of a cult of devil worshippers whose ceremonies called for blood and parts of animals. Others said the mutilations were the work of extraterrestrial beings from UFOs. The UFO theory quickly became the most popular.

An investigation by the South Dakota Crime Bureau determined that all the cattle had died of natural causes. The "mutilations" were really the work of small predators, such as weasels, that simply chewed off the softer parts of the dead animals. When the Crime Bureau made its announcement, reports of "mysterious" cattle mutilations virtually ceased in Nebraska and South Dakota. But by that time similar episodes were being reported in Texas, Colorado, Oklahoma, and Kansas. As before, the UFO explanation was a popular one.

There was a very similar cattle mutilation scare in Colorado back in 1968, and UFOs were mentioned in connection with that one too. Interest in it died within a few weeks, but interest in the scare that began in 1974 in Nebraska and South Dakota has continued to grow over the years.

In the area where I live there are few cattle, but a number of dead dogs have been found. No one seems to know where the dogs came from or why they were killed. It is, as of this writing, a genuine and gruesome mystery. And people are saying that UFOs are somehow responsible.

Chapter 17
THEORIES BEYOND SPACE

A FEW YEARS AGO, while I was reading a book called *The Fairy-Faith in Celtic Countries,* I ran across an interesting statement in the introduction, which was written by Leslie Shepard. He reported that in Britain there is a Fairy Investigation Society that collects accounts of fairy sightings in much the same way UFO organizations collect stories of UFO sightings. "In their 1963 Newsletter, they reported some fascinating fairy viewing in Buckinghampshire."

Shepard continued, "I have a strong suspicion that in the newer mythology of flying saucers, some of those 'shining visitors' in spacecraft from other worlds might turn out to be just another form of fairies."

I thought the idea quaint and charming. But had I suggested, even in jest, that serious Ufologists might say such things I would have been accused of slandering their good name. The crazy contactees, of course, could be accused of saying anything, but certainly not the solid and sane folk with advanced degrees in science.

So you can imagine my surprise when I sat down with a copy of *Passport to Magonia* by Jacques Vallee—master's degree in astrophysics, Ph.D. in computer science, author of several pro-UFO books, a close associate of Dr. J. Allen Hynek, and generally one of the more prestigious of modern Ufologists—and found myself reading about fairies and flying saucers. Vallee states as his "basic contention" that "the modern, global belief in flying saucers and their occupants is identical to an earlier belief in the fairy faith."

It is all part of a major move away from the old nuts-and-bolts, "UFOs are spaceships from other planets" belief that dominated the early years of Ufology. Though no surveys have been taken on the question, I feel quite certain that the bulk of those who believe in UFOs, particularly those who have a rather casual belief, would still hold fast to the extraterrestrial hypothesis. But among those who, like Vallee, are deeply involved in the subject, the extraterrestrial explanation has been losing ground to ever more exotic theories. In this chapter we will examine some of these theories.

The late Ivan Sanderson began his career as a naturalist and nature writer, but he spent most of his later years writing about Fortean subjects like Bigfoot and UFOs. Sanderson advanced a couple of fairly complicated theories about what UFOs really are. For some unaccountable reason (probably out of sheer perversity), Sanderson chose to call them Unexplained Aerial Objects or UAOs. His theories were highly tentative, and it is difficult to assess how seriously he took them or anything else he said. But serious or not, Ivan Sanderson could never be accused of lacking in imagination.

In his book *Uninvited Visitors*, published in 1967, Sanderson put forth the idea that his UAOs might be "living machines," some sort of advanced biological creations adapted to living in space, or perhaps even the products of natural cosmic evolution. He wrote:

> It is my contention that at least some of the UAOs that have visited us in the past, and are now still visiting this planet, are indeed constructions manufactured by intelligent entities, but they are not "machines" as we think of them. But here our inquiry gets really complicated, because we find ourselves confronted with a considerable number of alternatives.

First, we must face the possibility of "machines" constructed along biological lines, and possibly copied from already existing life forms that had already overcome certain basic problems of life in "space" and of movement through it. Second, we must also face up to the possibility of intelligences constructing what we would otherwise call "animals" or new "life forms" either by breeding them—as we do dogs, cattle, etc.—or by purely biochemical means, as by manipulating the macromolecules that, like DNA, carry the "pattern" for the life form that is to develop from an ovum or other primary source.

This biological theory of UFOs didn't attract much attention, and indeed it was not entirely original—the idea of "living UFOs" had been floated before. So a few years later Sanderson came back with another theory, which proved to be considerably more popular. In his book *Invisible Residents,* which came out in 1970, Sanderson discussed all sorts of mysteries of the sea, such as the Bermuda Triangle. He also said that 50 percent of all UFO sightings "have been recorded as coming out of, going into, appearing from over, or disappearing over water." Such an observation hardly seems surprising, considering that over 70 percent of the surface of the earth is covered with water and that a considerable percentage of the world's population lives near some body of water. Still, Sanderson insisted that UFOs had an affinity to water.

In this Sanderson saw an "underlying unity" that made him conclude that all sea mysteries are part of an "overall concept." What was this "overall concept"?

Simply that there is an underwater "civilization" (or civilizations) on this planet that has been here for a very long time and has evolved here, and/or that there are intelligent entities who have been coming here from elsewhere, probably for a very

134 THE WORLD OF UFOS

long time, and prefer to use the bottom of the hydrosphere
[that is, the bottom of the sea].

Now, in the end this is not so very different from Richard
Shaver's and Ray Palmer's underground world (see Chapter
16), but placing the unknown civilization under the sea was
definitely a new wrinkle. At least I think it was, but so many
UFO theories have been kicked around over the years that I
simply may have missed that one before Sanderson popular-
ized it.

Sanderson also tackled head-on two of the most vexing problems of Ufology: why UFOs and their occupants seem to en-
gage in entirely illogical, apparently random activities; and
how it could be that UFOs often seem to violate basic laws of
physics. UFOs appear to missionaries in New Guinea or to
businessmen flying over Washington state, but not to scientists
who might be able to understand what they are doing, or to
recognized governmental authorities. The little men get out
and kidnap people in the White Mountains or dig up bits of soil
in New Jersey, when it seems that by this time they ought to
know what human beings and earthly soil are like. They are
often seen yet remain elusive. They can appear and disappear
suddenly. They fly at fantastic speeds and make "impossible"
turns. In short, the pattern of UFO observations makes no
sense to us at all.

Why should it? Sanderson asks. Since these "things," whatever they may be, are so much more advanced than we are,
we really have no way of figuring out what they are doing, or
why. They may be, in Sanderson's words, "overcivilized and
quite mad." They may have so much technology at their command that "they could live anywhere or everywhere, and
move about instantly, or faster, anywhere throughout space
and/or time."

Like the statement "The ways of the gods are unknowable,"

this theory explains everything by insisting that nothing can be explained. Which doesn't get us anywhere, but does show that Ivan Sanderson was never at a loss for something to say about UFOs.

A significant contribution to Ufological theory was made back in the late 1950s by the famed Swiss psychoanalyst Dr. Carl Gustav Jung. Jung had once been Sigmund Freud's chief disciple, and later became the chief Freudian heretic. Jung developed a worldwide following all his own, and his statements on any subject were bound to be regarded with great interest.

In 1954 a magazine article quoted Jung as saying some things that tended to identify him as a believer in UFOs. Later he wrote a book called *Flying Saucers: A Modern Myth of Things Seen in the Sky;* this was supposed to clarify his position on UFOs.

Now, Jung's works are very difficult to understand, but they are supposed to be extremely profound. Most people are afraid to comment on them for fear that they have misunderstood something vital and will be thought foolish. So for years most Ufologists seemed to think that Jung believed in the same kind of UFOs that they did—real, material spaceships.

Well, maybe he did, though he admitted in his book that he had no training in the physical sciences and was therefore unable to deal adequately with the possibility of the physical reality of the objects. Still, one does get the impression that Jung, like any good UFO buff, did believe in real, material spaceships—though one can never be sure, and it isn't terribly important. What Jung did that was important to later Ufological theory was to deal with the "psychic aspects" of UFOs.

Jung thought that UFOs were important because belief in them had become so widespread that they had become "a living myth." He thought that the belief in UFOs sprang from very deep causes, and that whether UFOs were a physical reality or not, they were significant and deserved further study.

Back in the 1950s, when people expected real spaceships to land at any moment, talk of "living myths" and "psychic projections" was pretty thin soup. But as time went on and the spaceships did not land, and no hard physical evidence of spaceships could be turned up, Jung's thin soup began to look more nourishing. Today a lot of people who began as nuts-and-bolts Ufologists are talking about UFOs as living myths and psychic projections. The once despised contactees are being given a new look by the sort of people who earlier would have regarded them as screwballs and distractions on the road to true knowledge.

Aside from the disappointing lack of physical evidence for the existence of spaceships, times have also changed. The space program doesn't command public attention as it once did. There is a great deal of talk about altered consciousness and other realities. A motto for many present-day seekers of new truths is this statement by Dr. John Lilly: "What one believes to be true either is true or becomes true in one's mind." This new atmosphere has affected the world of UFOs.

So it was that in 1969 I found Jacques Vallee discussing UFOs as a "living myth" in *Passport to Magonia*. Though Vallee never quite comes out and says it, he does seem to believe that there is a physical reality behind both fairy lore and UFO sightings. He tentatively concludes that mankind has long been in contact with a secretive superior race; the beings may come from another universe or another dimension, and the physical reality in which they live is surely not the same as ours. This is an old science-fiction concept and, appropriately enough, Vallee has been a science-fiction writer.

In a book called *The Edge of Reality*, which is really the transcription of a series of tape-recorded conversations between Vallee, J. Allen Hynek, and psychologist Arthur C. Hastings, we find Hynek saying:

> All of these things [psychic phenomena] are pointing out or signaling that there's a reality that the physical scientists, the Condons, the Menzels, aren't at all conscious of, but exists! . . .
> Should these psychic claims be true, it opens up another can of worms. Then the problem essentially is solved; that explains why UFOs can make right-angle turns, that explains why they can be dematerialized, why sometimes they are picked up on radar and sometimes not, and why they are not detected by our infrared equipment. All that. But that's dangerous territory to tread.

Dangerous or not, Dr. Hynek has been treading that territory more frequently of late. He has become a regular participant at psychic conferences where such matters as "spiritual healing" and "communications with unseen worlds" are discussed for the benefit of audiences of believers. At a 1977 UFO conference Hynek talked of the possibility of parallel universes. It seems a long way from the UFOs of old, and an even longer way from swamp gas.

While Ufologists have gotten more and more interested in psychic matters, psychics have become more UFO-minded. Of course, contactees always talked about getting "psychic power" from the space people, but in the past most big-time psychics did not go heavily into the world of UFOs.

However, Uri Geller, the popular metal-bending psychic, claimed that he was getting information from superintelligences from the planet Hoova, and that he had been contacted by beings from a UFO. Or at least that's what it seemed for a while. This and other equally startling things were reported in a biography of Geller written by Dr. Andriji Puharich. Dr.

Puharich was the man who originally brought Geller to the United States, and he was in a large measure responsible for Geller's enormous fame in the early 1970s. But the stories about Hoova and the UFOs didn't go down very well with Geller's fans, and while he never actually denied the Puharich account, he didn't exactly endorse it either. The once close relationship between the pair seems to have cooled considerably.

Puharich insists that everything he wrote is Geller gospel. He told writer Brad Steiger:

> When Uri found out that people did not like the idea of Spectra [a cosmic supercomputer] and Hoova, he chose to deny them at a point that is well marked in time—in January of 1974, when he realized that his speaking of them might hurt his show-business career. From that moment he began to backpedal.
>
> But, believe me, he was a witness to every event. We've seen the spacecraft. He's photographed them. I've photographed them. I've seen him go aboard them, and we've all been in the same place.

Ingo Swann, another popular psychic, claims to have taken out-of-the-body trips around the planets under the supervision of the National Aeronautics and Space Administration. Naturally, NASA denies it all.

More than psychics have gotten into Ufology. When I met F. W. (Ted) Holiday at Loch Ness in 1966, he was a perfectly ordinary monster buff. He was out there at the loch with his cameras, absolutely convinced that he was going to get a photograph of the great beast that he knew lived in the murky depths. Yet in his 1973 book, *The Dragon and the Disc,* he links the Loch Ness monster, fairies, UFOs, and the paranormal in some cosmic scheme that, frankly, I was unable to fathom.

Probably the two farthest-out major theoreticians now putting forth paranormal or paraphysical explanations for UFOs are John Keel and Jacques Vallee.

Keel, who spent a lot of time tramping around West Virginia looking for Mothman and talking to people who had talked to people in UFOs, finally decided that it's all connected—monsters, UFOs, religious miracles, the Men in Black, ancient gods, practically everything that somebody has believed in but has not been able to prove. None of them, says Keel, can be taken at face value. They are all part of a grand deception.

Keel says that monsters, UFOs, etc. are "constructs" or "psychic projections" that are being foisted upon us by something that controls us and has always controlled us. What is this something? Well, that's hard to say. In some of Keel's earlier books it seemed as though this something was the space people. In his latest book, *The Eighth Tower,* he talks about "the superspectrum," which is "the only reality." But just what the superspectrum is supposed to be escapes me, and it escapes many who are more sympathetic readers of his books than I. It seems to be something like the cosmic mind, or God, but I wouldn't swear to that explanation. Anyway, it's not the little green men from Mars.

Vallee is, if anything, even less clear in the speculations contained in *The Invisible College.* The Invisible College of the title, by the way, is supposed to be a sort of underground organization of about one hundred scientists and scholars in half a dozen countries who are engaged in studying the problems raised by UFOs. They are supposed to have access to all sorts of information denied scientists and scholars outside the magic circle, and certainly denied the general public. Who the members of this Invisible College are, Vallee does not say. He is a member, certainly, and presumably his friend Dr. Hynek is too, but as to the others, and how they get their information, we are left quite in the dark.

In *The Invisible College,* Vallee seems to be groping for a religious explanation for UFOs. He speaks of "the appearance of new faiths centered on the UFO belief." And he ends on this rather scary but distinctly mystic note:

> It is not simply our freedom that is in danger now. It is a certain concept of humanity. And it is no longer to science that we must turn to understand the nature of this psychic crisis and find its key. Nor will the answer be discovered in some secret file in Washington. The solution lies where it has always been: *within ourselves.* We can reach it any time we want.

Remember, now, that he started out talking about UFOs.

It has often been observed that religious wars are the most brutal. That is perhaps why a dispute between Vallee and Keel has assumed such a nasty tone. Keel, who has a prickly temper anyway, has accused Vallee and others of simply plagiarizing his work. Vallee's friend Aime Michael, another French Ufologist, has responded that Vallee has held these ideas for years and often used them in the science-fiction novels he has published in France under various pen names.

Actually, very similar ideas have also been around in the United States for quite a while. Back in the late '50s and early '60s, a fellow who wrote under the pen name Peter Kor wrote a regular column for a little publication called *Saucer News.* Kor put out many of these same esoteric ideas. But *Saucer News* was for the hard-core true believer and had a circulation, at its height, of only a few hundred. Science fiction is science fiction. Now ideas from science fiction are being presented seriously to a wide audience, and that represents a distinct change in atmosphere.

The psychic, the paraphysical, or whatever you choose to call it should bulk very large in the world of UFOs in the years to come.

Chapter 18
NEW AGE PROPHETS

JACQUES VALLEE HAS WRITTEN of "the appearance of new faiths centered on the UFO belief." Of course, there have been "new faiths" ("cults" to those who dislike them) based on UFO beliefs practically since the beginning. Moreover, Ufological ideas have become part of the fabric of modern occultism. Practically no new esoteric religion can escape some brush with UFOs.

Some older religions, too, have taken up the UFO idea. The Divine Light Mission—a Hindu group that had a brief but spectacular rise (and equally spectacular fall) in the United States under the leadership of its teenaged "Perfect Master," Guru Maharaj-Ji—took up UFOs. In 1973 the guru's followers held a huge festival in the Houston Astrodome. There were dead serious rumors that a UFO was going to land at the Astrodome, presumably to give the approval of the space people to the event. There were even spaces reserved in the Astrodome parking lot for the UFO.

Needless to say, no UFO ever landed. The festival itself was a bust, and the Divine Light Mission went into a steep decline. Some of those who attended the festival felt that it was hurt by "the UFO business."

Most orthodox Christian groups stay far away from speculations about UFOs, although some of the more apocalyptic-minded may speak of UFOs as another "sign" of the coming Last Days. Others seem to regard interest in UFOs as being satanically inspired.

Far and away the most widely publicized UFO religious

movement of the last few years—indeed, probably the most widely publicized Ufological event of any kind of the last few years—was the promised UFO trip of a couple of "illuminated" contactees who call themselves Bo and Peep.

In the fall of 1975, newspapers throughout the country reported that somewhere between a dozen and twenty people had "disappeared" from a small Oregon town. They had not been kidnapped, but had been told by a mysterious couple that if they left everything behind they would be taken up on a spaceship to something or someplace known as "the next level above human."

The tale even received national TV coverage on the October 8 CBS Evening News broadcast, making it the first UFO-related story to hit national TV news in a long time. In the beginning, the whole thing sounded very sinister; people leaving home and family to join up with—what? A band of murderers, thieves, drug addicts? But when the details finally came out, it was clear that nothing sinister was going on. The whole story was just strange, and also very, very typical of one part of the world of UFOs.

Brad Steiger, a prolific writer on Ufological subjects, interviewed the mysterious couple (who called themselves "the Two" when they weren't calling themselves Bo and Peep) early in 1975, before they became national news. He had been put in contact with them by Hayden Hewes of the International UFO Bureau, a long-time Ufologist. Hewes was to do a foreword for a book that Bo and Peep were writing.

Steiger found the couple "physically attractive but certainly unprepossessing individuals, clad informally in lumberjack shirts and casual slacks—two very sincere, soft-spoken individuals who appeared to be totally involved in their work and totally committed to what they considered their mission here on Earth."

Steiger's interview with Bo and Peep, published in his book

Gods of Aquarius, provides no details on the background of the mysterious pair, and indeed provides little information on what their "mission" is supposed to be. Steiger does make the observation that their message is heavily Christian, and similar to that given by other contactees.

The Two seem to believe that in addition to being picked up by a UFO, they and their followers will undergo some sort of physical or chemical transformation. They told Steiger:

> The only conversion experience we're interested in is that of the physical anatomy, the biological and chemical changeover from human-level creature to a creature in the next evolutionary level.
>
> Just as the caterpillar has to cease all his caterpillar activities in order to enter his chrysalis, so must the same thing happen to a human who says, "The only desire I have is to make this transition. Therefore, I am going to rise above and overcome all of my human desires and activities and emerge an individual that can enter a physically different realm from the human altogether."

After they became well known, James S. Phelan, a West Coast writer, caught up with the Two "by a process too Byzantine to relate." They agreed to an interview in Little Rock, Arkansas, where they happened to be staying at the time. They and their little flock had been wandering about for some months and had dropped out of sight of the major news media.

Phelan wrote an article about the Two that was published in *The New York Times Magazine* on February 29, 1976. This report provides more details about the couple and the movement they began.

Bo—whose real, or earthly, name is Marshall Herff Applewhite—is a musician and former professor of music. Peep is

Bonnie Lu Trousdale Nettles, a professional nurse. Both are Texans with interests in astrology, reincarnation, and other occult subjects. They met at a Houston hospital in 1972 and immediately became convinced that they had known each other in previous lives.

Not long after this they had a sort of collective "illumination" in which they realized they had come from "the level above human" and had a mission to "awaken" people on Earth. One of the messages they had to give to people was that they could be taken aboard a UFO and transported to heaven.

The Two are reluctant to talk about their past, because they think it detracts from their message. "That is why we took such stupid names."

Bo and Peep admit that they were somewhat nervous about making the announcement about their mission and the UFO. They told Phelan, "There was a little Episcopal church in Spokane, Washington. We wrote on the register at the church what our mission was and then ran. Next we told a Baptist preacher in Oklahoma City, and he threw us out. He said he had had Moses and Elijah there and didn't need anyone else. After that we wrote little notes about our mission and dropped them in the strangest places all over the nation. I'm sure people have found them in the middle of their Bibles."

Bo and Peep never made much headway in the regular churches, though both come from traditional Christian backgrounds and their message has a strong overlay of Christianity. They only began to pick up an appreciative audience when they moved into occult circles in Southern California. "There are a lot of advanced souls in Southern California," Bo said to Phelan.

They gathered some converts in Southern California and moved up the coast, spreading their message to small groups in private homes, on college campuses, and wherever else a group of listeners could be brought together. There is an informal but effective occult–Ufological grapevine, and when a couple of new personalities pass through, interested parties always know about them.

In Newport, Oregon, the Two held a meeting in a local motel. There, according to reports, some twenty people joined up for the UFO trip. Among them were a young couple who left their children behind. This was the incident that propelled a rather run-of-the-mill UFO cult into national prominence.

Phelan found that most of those who had chosen to follow the Two had already had occult and/or Ufological interests and had previously been members of other groups. Once they joined up, they engaged in something called the Process. That appeared to involve wandering about in small groups from campsite to campsite, occasionally spreading the word. In early 1976 the flock was estimated at between three hundred and one thousand; no one seemed to have an exact figure.

At first Bo and Peep seemed to promise their followers that the UFO pickup was imminent, that it might come within a year. That didn't happen, and Bo and Peep admit that setting a date was a mistake. But they haven't backed down on the UFO, which they still expect within a few years—or perhaps next week. The missed deadline, however, did cause some to defect, and left a residue of bitterness among former followers.

Little has been heard from Bo and Peep and their flock since 1976, and it is not unreasonable to assume that this group will disappear, as so many similar groups have in the past.

It was an accident of publicity that propelled Bo and Peep and their followers into brief national prominence. Many people expressed surprise that such a group could exist at all, or that seemingly intelligent and rational people could join up, even briefly. Yet there is no reason for surprise. Groups of believers in various UFO religions exist right now all over America, and in other countries as well. They are often deliberately secretive; others would love publicity, but simply have not struck the fancy of reporters as yet. There are many individuals who say they are getting essentially the same message Bo and Peep got, but they lack the talent or the luck to pick up followers.

In a way, Bo and Peep fit right into the mainstream of religious visionaries, ancient and modern. They consider themselves harbingers of the Last Days of the world as we know it. Brad Steiger points out that though Bo and Peep were "reluctant to enter the category of Doomsday prophets, there is something about the very nature of their quest that is certainly suggestive of the Last Days spoken of in the book of Revelation." There certainly is.

In The Revelation of St. John the Divine, a prophetic and difficult-to-interpret part of the New Testament that describes St. John's vision of the Last Days, there is a passage that tells of "two witnesses" with the power to prophesy, whose message "tormented them that dwelt on the earth."

According to the book of Revelation, the two witnesses are killed by unbelievers, lie unburied for three days, and then rise from the dead to heaven in a cloud, much to the consternation of their enemies and of scoffers generally.

Bo and Peep very definitely consider themselves to be the two witnesses spoken of in Revelation—that is why they sometimes call themselves the Two. They don't look forward to martyrdom, or the Demonstration, as they call it, but they are not seeking to avoid it either. Bo told James Phelan, "We would be pleased to have the Demonstration come quickly so we could go back into our Father's kingdom and go on with our work there, instead of here. . . . The world does not have to choose to do us in, but the chances that it won't happen are about as great as that a rain will wash all the red dirt out of Oklahoma."

Brad Steiger and others who have interviewed large numbers of contactees say that most of them are getting messages that Earth is now in its Last Days. This is not exactly a new development; if you recall, the people in the Minnesota UFO cult mentioned in Chapter 7 also expected End of the World cataclysms from which they would be rescued by a UFO, and that was in the 1960s. And in the '50s George Adamski and the other early contactees said that "the space brothers" were here to save us from a disastrous nuclear war. Most modern psychic prophets fall into the Doomsday category, predicting that the end of the world or something just short of it will come before the year 2000.

While many of the contactee prophets seem to be predicting a fiery end and a Last Judgment of the type described in the book of Revelation, others seem to express a more cheerful view. They see the trials and tribulations of the present day as the opening phase of a New Age, which will be just wonderful.

All sorts of things—UFOs, Christianity, astrology, occultism, and a great deal more—are mixed together in the message that the modern contactees say they are getting from the space people. But with the exception of UFOs, which are a new addition, these messages are very much the same as those received by psychics and prophets down through the ages. That is why skeptics and some Ufologists as well have come to look at UFO beliefs as just part of a much larger and older belief system.

Do these messages have any significance for us? It might be wise to reflect upon this: prophets have been saying that the end of the world is near for several thousand years now. There are dangers on every side of us—nuclear war, ecological disaster, natural catastrophes, just to name a few—and we have no reason to be complacent. But the world has never been a safe place, and despite repeated prophecies of the end, for better or worse, we are still here.

Chapter 19
QUO VADIS?

THE MYSTERY OF UFOS, if indeed there is a mystery at all, is no nearer solution now than it was in the days right after Kenneth Arnold's 1947 sighting. But that doesn't mean people have lost interest in UFOs—far from it.

Americans' interest in UFOs was at its lowest ebb in late 1968 and early 1969—these were the months preceding and following the publication of the Condon Report. The number of UFO sightings reported dropped off sharply after the Air Force closed down Project Blue Book in March, 1969, and there was no longer a central agency to report sightings to. Nationwide press publicity dropped to near zero.

But slowly interest began to build once again, until by 1973–74 UFO buffs were proclaiming that a full-scale "flap" or "wave" on the order of the ones in 1952 and 1966 was again upon us.

Some UFO theorists contend that there is a regular, cyclic pattern in the number of reported UFO sightings, though they can find no clear reason for the cycle. Critics, on the other hand, contend that one well-publicized sighting tends to focus the attention of press and public on the subject of UFOs. What happens then is *not* that people see more things in the sky that they cannot identify, but that they start identifying the things they see as spaceships. Such identifications, which under ordinary conditions would receive scant attention, are then often given considerable press play. In 1952 the key case was the Washington Airport radar sightings. In 1966 it was the Michigan "swamp gas" sightings. In 1973, the UFO event that received most attention was the alleged kidnapping at Pascagoula, Mississippi.

While the Air Force probably hoped that the Condon Report would end all scientific controversy over UFOs, UFO buffs now claim that Ufology is gaining respectability in the scientific community. They cite a recent survey by Dr. Peter A. Sturrock of Stanford University. Sturrock mailed questionnaires to members of the American Astronomical Society (AAS), and the majority of those who replied indicated that they believe the UFO problem deserves further study. This particular survey was given wide publicity.

The anti-UFO forces have objected to the survey and the interpretations put on it for numerous reasons. One is that Sturrock's previous pro-UFO activities were not identified in the publicity about the study, and that only pro-UFO people were consulted in preparing the questionnaire. For that reason, say the critics, some of the questions were loaded in a pro-UFO direction. Another criticism is that the results of the survey are not nearly as impressive as UFO buffs make them out to be. For one thing, many of the AAS members queried did not answer the questionnaire, and a follow-up questionnaire indicated that those who replied to the first survey were more pro-UFO than those who did not; thus, the survey does not give a true measure of the sentiments of the entire AAS membership. But in any case, only a tiny percentage of those who replied to Sturrock's questionnaire thought that UFOs were extraterrestrial in origin. The vast majority opted for more prosaic terrestrial explanations for UFO sightings. So, as with most surveys, the results of Dr. Sturrock's can be read in any number of different ways, depending on what you want to make out of them.

UFO publicity has picked up considerably since the late 1960s. Perhaps the most consistent and probably the most effective publicity organ for UFOs during the 1970s has been the tabloid *National Enquirer.* The *Enquirer,* which sells millions of copies at newsstands and supermarket checkout counters every week, regularly prints sensational UFO tales. The publication has offered prizes amounting to many thousands of dollars for "the best UFO case of the year." The publication retains regular UFO consultants and has a large budget to investigate UFO sightings. (You may recall that the *National Enquirer* got mixed up with the Travis Walton case discussed in Chapter 10.)

However, the *Enquirer* has a well-established reputation for sensationalism, and is not regarded as a serious newspaper by most members of the press. I even wonder how seriously many of its readers take what they read in its columns. I suspect that it is considered more of an entertainment medium than a source of information. In any event, the more serious Ufologists are slightly embarrassed by the championing of their cause by a publication that mixes UFO stories, celebrity gossip, and astrological predictions in about equal proportions.

While the Air Force is officially out of the UFO business, it has not entirely disappeared from the demonology of the Ufologist. The CIA most certainly has not. Rumors continually circulate that the CIA has long run a secret investigation that has turned up sensational, but secret, information.

William H. Spaulding, director of Ground Saucer Watch (GSW), one of the larger UFO organizations, told Alan Riding of *The New York Times:*

> The CIA says it hasn't worked on UFOs since 1953, and the Air Force says it stopped its project in 1969. But we have evidence that both are still working on the subject. We want congressional hearings to obtain the release of all information on UFOs obtained by American intelligence agencies.

The inauguration of President Jimmy Carter was greeted with considerable enthusiasm in some Ufological circles, for there was a report that Carter had sighted a UFO in Leary, Georgia, in 1960. Because of this—so the rumor went—the United States was going to adopt an entirely new and more open attitude toward UFOs. The Carter administration did ask the National Aeronautics and Space Administration to look into the possibility of reopening a UFO investigation. In December, 1977, NASA declined, saying there was no new evidence, so another investigation was not justified.

During the 1970s, UFO organizations, which had been on the decline for years, began to revive. NICAP, shaken by internal struggles and financial difficulties, never recovered its preeminent position among UFO groups. Perhaps this is because Donald Keyhoe had set uncovering the Air Force cover-up as NICAP's main job. Now, with the Air Force out of the UFO business (at least as far as anyone really knows) and its files open to all, the enemy is gone—NICAP's major *raison d'être* has disappeared. Still, NICAP is alive today, and regularly puts out a vigorous little publication called *UFO Investigator.*

During the early 1970s the Midwest UFO Network (MUFON), started in 1969, prospered enormously—probably because of its close association with Dr. J. Allen Hynek. For Hynek, the circle has become complete. He has moved from what his enemies considered an Air Force apologist to what his enemies on the other side call "the spiritual leader of the UFO believers." One small UFO magazine recently printed a drawing of Hynek and under it the motto "In God we trust."

Perhaps the most significant new organization to be formed during the early '70s was Hynek's own Center for UFO Studies (CUFOS). It came into being late in 1973. According to Hynek, CUFOS is an outgrowth of the Invisible College. Most of the members appear to be scientists and technicians, and it is not open to general membership, though it does maintain a close relationship with MUFON. The organization has a toll-free number for reporting sightings, but it is known only to police departments, planetariums, and the like, not to the general public. CUFOS would like to serve as a central clearinghouse for all UFO reports, but lacks the funds to investigate more than a selected few.

Phil Klass has accused CUFOS of being essentially a one-man operation, that man being J. Allen Hynek. This Hynek vigorously denies. But there can be little doubt that Hynek is now the leading figure not only in CUFOS, but in the entire world of "serious Ufology."

In late 1976, a new publication, the *International UFO Reporter,* was begun under Hynek's editorship. It is a small but highly professional-looking publication that provides information on UFO events from around the world. For his first issue, Hynek wrote a "Declaration of Principles" that reads, in part:

> To treat the UFO "scene," the flow of reports, as the global phenomenon it is, but quite separately from theories advanced to explain the phenomenon. Since the most popular current hypothesis by far is the "extraterrestrial visitation," it must not be allowed to obfuscate the open study of the phenomenon. There might be *another* answer—even several answers!

The UFO skeptics have not remained unorganized either. In June, 1977, the Committee for the Scientific Investigation of Claims of the Paranormal formed a subcommittee on UFOs; it is headed by that arch-opponent of UFO believers, Phil Klass. Klass's two associate directors are James Oberg, an editor of *Space World,* which was once published by (of all people) Ray Palmer; and Robert Scheaffer, a computer analyst and a former student of (of all people) J. Allen Hynek. After thirty years, members of the Ufological community have begun tripping over one another.

On the formation of the committee, Klass said:

> Because our investigations must be conducted in our spare time, we cannot respond to numerous reports of seemingly

mysterious "lights in the night sky" that turn out to be Venus or other celestial bodies, a hoax hot-air balloon, or to have other prosaic explanations. Instead we will concentrate on major cases that have been analyzed by experienced investigators and have been hailed as defying prosaic/terrestrial explanation.

So the lines are drawn, and we can expect some rousing fights in the future.

A BRIEF POSTSCRIPT: On August 15, 1977, shortly after the manuscript of this book was completed, Ray Palmer, the original flying-saucer buff, and in many ways the hero of this book, died. Three months before his death Palmer made a rare public appearance at a thirtieth-anniversary UFO convention held in Chicago and sponsored by *Fate* magazine. Palmer regaled a large and appreciative audience with his wild theories about UFOs and the hollow earth. Then he warned them not to necessarily take everything, or anything, he said seriously. He was a man who knew how to enjoy UFOs.

SELECTED BIBLIOGRAPHY

Adamski, George. *Behind the Flying Saucer Mystery.* New York: Warner Books, 1974.

———. *Inside the Space Ships.* New York: Abelard-Schuman, 1955.

Barker, Gray. *They Knew Too Much About Flying Saucers.* New York: University Books, 1956.

Bender, Albert K. *Flying Saucers and the Three Men in Black.* London: Neville Spearman, 1963.

Bernard, Raymond. T. *The Hollow Earth.* New York: University Books, 1969.

Blum, Ralph, and Blum, Judy. *Beyond Earth: Man's Contact with UFOs.* New York: Bantam Books, 1976.

Cohen, Daniel. *The Ancient Visitors.* New York: Doubleday & Co., 1976.

Condon, Edward U., ed. *Scientific Study of Unidentified Flying Objects.* New York: Bantam Books, 1969.

Dione, Robert I. *God Drives a Flying Saucer.* New York: Bantam Books, 1973.

Edwards, Frank. *Flying Saucers—Serious Business.* New York: Bantam Books, 1966.

Festinger, Leon, et al. *When Prophecy Fails.* Minneapolis: University of Minnesota Press, 1966.

Flammonde, Paris. *The Age of Flying Saucers.* New York: Hawthorn Books, 1971.

Flindt, Max H., and Binder, Otto O. *Mankind—Child of the Stars.* New York: Fawcett World Library, 1974.

Fort, Charles. *The Books of Charles Fort.* New York: Dover Publications, 1975.

Fuller, John. *Aliens in the Skies.* New York: G. P. Putnam's Sons, 1969.

———. *Incident at Exeter.* New York: Berkley Books, 1966.

———. *The Interrupted Journey.* New York: Berkley Books, 1974.

Hall, Richard, ed. *The UFO Evidence.* Washington, D.C.: National Investigations Committee for Aerial Phenomena, 1964.

Holiday, F. W. *The Dragon and the Disc.* New York: W. W. Norton & Co., 1973.

Hynek, J. Allen. *The UFO Experience: A Scientific Inquiry.* Chicago: Henry Regnery Co., 1972.

Hynek, J. Allen, and Vallee, Jacques. *The Edge of Reality.* Chicago: Henry Regnery Co., 1975.

Jacobs, David Michael. *The UFO Controversy in America.* Bloomington, Ind.: University of Indiana Press, 1975.

Jung, Carl G. *Flying Saucers: A Modern Myth of Things Seen in the Sky.* New York: Harcourt Brace, 1959.

Keel, John. *The Eighth Tower.* New York: Saturday Review Press, 1976.

———. *The Mothman Prophecies.* New York: Saturday Review Press, 1975.

———. *Our Haunted Planet.* New York: Fawcett World Library, 1971.

———. *Strange Creatures from Time and Space.* New York: Fawcett World Library, 1970.

———. *UFOs: Operation Trojan Horse.* New York: G. P. Putnam's Sons, 1970.

Keyhoe, Donald. *Aliens from Space.* New York: Doubleday & Co., 1973.

———. *The Flying Saucer Conspiracy.* New York: Holt, Rinehart & Winston, 1955.

———. *The Flying Saucers Are Real.* New York: Fawcett World Library, 1950.

———. *Flying Saucers from Outer Space.* New York: Holt, Rinehart & Winston, 1953.

———. *Flying Saucers: Top Secret.* New York: G. P. Putnam's Sons, 1960.

Klass, Philip J. *UFOs Explained.* New York: Random House, 1975.

———. *UFOs Identified.* New York: Random House, 1968.

Knight, Damon. *Charles Fort, Prophet of the Unexplained.* New York: Doubleday & Co., 1970.

Leslie, Desmond, and Adamski, George. *The Flying Saucers Have Landed.* New York: British Book Centre, 1962.

Lore, Gordon I. R., and Deneault, Harold H. *Mysteries of the Skies.* Englewood Cliffs, N.J.: Prentice-Hall, 1970.

Lorenzen, Coral, and Lorenzen, Jim. *Encounters with UFO Occupants.* New York: Berkley Books, 1976.

————. *Flying Saucers: The Startling Evidence of the Invasion from Outer Space.* New York: Signet Books, 1966.

Menzel, Donald, and Boyd, Lyle G. *The World of Flying Saucers.* New York: Doubleday & Co., 1963.

Nebel, John. *The Psychic World Around Us.* New York: Hawthorn Books, 1969.

Ruppelt, Edward J. *The Report on Unidentified Flying Objects.* New York: Doubleday & Co., 1956.

Sagan, Carl, and Page, Thornton, eds. *UFOs: A Scientific Debate.* Ithaca, N.Y.: Cornell University Press, 1973.

Sanderson, Ivan. *Invisible Residents.* New York: Avon Books, 1973.

————. *Uninvited Visitors.* Chicago: Henry Regnery Co., 1967.

Saunders, Howard, and Harkins, Roger. *UFOs—Yes! Where the Condon Committee Went Wrong.* New York: Signet Books, 1968.

Scully, Frank. *Behind the Flying Saucers.* New York: Holt, Rinehart & Winston, 1950.

Steiger, Brad. *Gods of Aquarius.* New York: Harcourt Brace Jovanovich, 1976.

Tomas, Andrew. *We Are Not the First.* New York: Bantam Books, 1973.

Vallee, Jacques. *Anatomy of a Phenomenon.* Chicago: Henry Regnery Co., 1969.

————. *The Invisible College.* New York: E. P. Dutton & Co., 1976.

————. *Passport to Magonia.* Chicago: Henry Regnery Co., 1969.

Vallee, Jacques, and Vallee, Janine. *Challenge to Science: The UFO Enigma.* Chicago: Henry Regnery Co., 1966.

von Däniken, Erich. *Chariots of the Gods?* New York: G. P. Putnam's Sons, 1970.

————. *Gods from Outer Space.* New York: G. P. Putnam's Sons, 1971.

————. *The Gold of the Gods.* New York: G. P. Putnam's Sons, 1973.

————. *In Search of Ancient Gods.* New York: G. P. Putnam's Sons, 1974.

Young, Mort. *UFO: Top Secret.* New York: Simon and Schuster, 1967.

INDEX

Adamski, George, 50–54, 114, 147
Aerial Phenomena Research Organization (APRO), 71, 79, 80
Air Force, 27–34, 150; CIA and, 32–33; Condon Committee and, 104–15, 148, 149; cover-up charges and, 42–49, 101; Florida scoutmaster incident and, 59–61; "invasion" of Washington, D.C., and, 36–41; Project Blue Book, 28, 34, 36, 70, 96, 114, 115; Project Grudge, 31, 33; Project Sign, 28–30, 33; secrecy and, 29–31, 33; Socorro incident and, 69–70
Allende, Carlos (Carl Allen), 129
American Association for the Advancement of Science (AAAS), 114–15
American Astronomical Society (AAS), 149
Anatomy of a Phenomenon (Vallee), 66, 67
Ancient accounts, 14–15
Ancient-astronaut theory, 116–24
Angelucci, Orfeo, 55
Applewhite, Marshall Herff (Bo), 142–46
Arnold, Kenneth, 21–25, 28, 116
Australian Flying Saucer Review, The, 67
Autobiography of Malcolm X, The, 65
Aviation Week and Space Technology, 70

Balloons, 23, 26–27, 36
Barker, Gray, 63, 87, 91, 123
Behind the Flying Saucers (Scully), 48
Bender, Albert K., 62–63
Bermuda Triangle, 127–28
Bernard, Raymond T., 126
Bethurum, Truman, 54
Bible, 14, 146
Bible and the Flying Saucers, The (Downing), 121
Big Flap, 35–41
Bo and Peep (the Two), 142–46
Broman, Francis, 48
Broshears, Raymond, 124
Brown, Harold, 101–02
Bug-Eyed Monsters (BEMs), 91
Byrd, Richard E., 126–27

Calf-napping hoax, 15–18
California sightings, 35, 92
Carter, Jimmy, 150–51
Case for the UFO, The (Jessup), 129
Cattle-mutilation incident, 130
Center for UFO Studies (CUFOS), 151–52
Chariots of the Gods? (von Däniken), 116–21
Chicago sighting, 35
Childhood's End (Clarke), 118
Chiles, Clarence S., 25–26
CIA, 32–33, 35, 150
Clark, Jerome, 16–18, 65
Clarke, Arthur C., 118

157

Colorado, University of, 103, 105
Committee for the Scientific Investigation of Claims of the Paranormal, 152
Condon Committee, 104–15, 148, 149
Condon, Edward U., 103–04, 106, 107, 109, 110, 112–14
Congressional hearings, 101–02, 108–09
Contactees, 50–57; dangerous UFOs and, 58–61; encounters of the third kind, 66–73; kidnappings, 74–80; Men in Black (MIB) and, 61–65, 127; monsters and, 87–93; in religious movements, 141–47
Contactee syndrome, 61, 62
Corddry, Charles, 28, 31
Crisman, Fred, 24–25, 122–23

Dahl, Harold, 24–25
Dangerous UFOs, 58–65
Divine Light Mission, 141
Dragon and the Disc, The (Holiday), 138

Edge of Reality, The, 136
Eighth Tower, The (Keel), 139
Encounters of the third kind, 66–73
Encounters with UFO Occupants (Lorenzen and Lorenzen), 92
European sightings, 20
Exeter (N.H.) sighting, 99
Ezekiel, 14

Fairy-Faith in Celtic Countries, The, 131
Fate, 10, 16–17, 22, 51
Ferrie, David W., 124
Flatwoods monster, 87–88
Florida scoutmaster incident, 58–61
Flying-saucer crash story, 48–49
Flying Saucers Have Landed, The (Adamski and Leslie), 52–53

Flying Saucers: A Modern Myth of Things Seen in the Sky (Jung), 135
Flying Saucers and the Three Men in Black (Bender), 63
"Foo fighters," 19–20
Ford, Gerald, 101
Fort, Charles, 19, 118
Fort Lee (N.J.) sighting, 71–72
Fredericks, Jennings, 90–91
Freiberg, Libby and Warren, 72–73
Fry, Daniel, 54–55
Fuller, John, 99–101, 107–09

Gallup Poll, 98
Garrison, Jim, 122–24
Geller, Uri, 137–38
Ghost rockets, 20, 27
Giant Rock Convention, 55
Gods of Aquarius (Steiger), 143
Gorman, George F., 26
Green, Gabriel, 55
Ground Saucer Watch (GSW), 150–51

Hallucinations, 19, 20
Hamilton, Alexander, 16–18
Hastings, Arthur C., 137
Hearst, William Randolph, 18
Hickson, Charles, 77–78, 87
Hill, Betty and Barney, 74–77, 101
Hillsdale College, 95–98
Hoaxes, 15–19, 24–25, 31, 58–61
Holiday, F. W. (Ted), 138
Hollow Earth, The (Bernard), 126
Hollow-earth theory, 125–26
House Armed Services Committee, 101–02
House Science and Astronautics Committee, 108
Hynek, J. Allen, 66, 67, 69, 78, 96–98, 101, 104, 105, 109, 113, 116, 131, 137, 139, 151–52

Incident at Exeter (Fuller), 100, 101
Inside the Space Ships (Adamski), 54

International Flying Saucer Bureau (IFSB), 62, 63
International UFO Reporter, 152
Interrupted Journey, The (Fuller), 74–77, 101
Invisible College, The (Vallee), 139–40
Invisible Residents (Sanderson), 133

Jacobs, David Michael, 18–19, 31
Jessup, Morris K., 63–64, 129
Jung, Carl Gustav, 135–36

Keel, John, 61, 64–65, 87, 89–90, 138–40
Kennedy assassination, 122–24
Keyhoe, Donald E., 43–47, 94, 100, 101, 104, 106, 115, 151
Kidnappings, 74–80
Klass, Phil, 70–71, 78–80, 101, 128, 152–53

Living myths, 135–36
Look, 100, 107, 108
Lorenzen, Coral, 71, 92
Lorenzen, Jim, 71, 79, 92
Louisville sighting, 22
Low, Robert, 105–07

McDonald, James E., 64, 106–08, 113
Mankind—Child of the Stars (Flindt and Binder), 121
Mannor, Frank, 95
Mantell, Thomas, 23–24, 42, 58
Maury Island incident, 24–25, 42–43, 58, 62, 122, 123
Men in Black (MIB), 61–65, 127
Menzel, Donald, 21, 105
Michael, Aime, 140
Michigan sightings, 95–98
Middle Ufology, 72
Midwest UFO Network (MUFON), 73, 115, 151
Monsters, 87–93

Moseley, Jim, 72–73
Mothman, 88–90
Mothman Prophecies, The (Keel), 64
Muscarello, Norman, 99

National Aeronautics and Space Administration, 138, 151
National Center for Atmospheric Research, 103
National Enquirer, 79, 150
National Investigations Committee for Aerial Phenomena (NICAP), 44, 54, 70, 80, 94, 99, 115, 151
National Science Association, 110–12
Navy, 23, 27, 30, 129
Nazca drawings, 118–20
Nettles, Bonnie Lu Trousdale (Peep), 142–46
Newfoundland sighting, 35
New Guinea sighting, 66–67
Newton, Silas, 48
New York Times Magazine, The, 143
Nixon, Richard, 104, 110, 114

O'Barski, George, 71–72, 74
Oberg, James, 152
Official UFO, 76
Oswald, Lee Harvey, 122

Palmer, Raymond A., 9, 10, 16, 21–22, 24, 25, 42–43, 123–27, 134, 152, 153
Parker, Calvin, 77–78, 87
Pascagoula (Miss.) kidnapping, 77–79, 87
Passport to Magonia (Vallee), 131, 136
Phelan, James S., 143–45, 146
"Philadelphia experiment," 129
Planetoid 127, 54
Plasma theory, 101, 128
Polar-hole theory, 126–27
Power failures, 128
Project Blue Book, 28, 34, 36, 70, 96, 114, 115
Project Grudge, 31, 33

Project Sign, 28–30, 33
Prophets, 141–47
Psychic phenomena, 135–40
Puharich, Andriji, 137–38

Questions and Answers by the Royal Order of Tibet (Adamski), 50–51
Quintanilla, Hector, 96–97

Religious movements, 141–47
Report on Unidentified Flying Objects, The (Ruppelt), 34
Robertson, H. P., 32
Robertson Panel, 32–33, 35, 47
Roush, Edward, 108
Ruppelt, Edward J., 28–29, 34–38, 47

Sagan, Carl, 76
Samford, John A., 39–41, 47
Sanderson, Ivan, 132–34
Saturday Evening Post, 31, 43
Saturday Review, 99, 100
Saucer News, 140
Saunders, David, 105–07, 109
Scheaffer, Robert, 76, 77, 152
Science, 107
Scully, Frank, 48, 100
Shaver Mystery, 123–25
Shaver, Richard S., 123–25, 134
Shaw, Clay L., 122, 123
Shepard, Leslie, 131
Skyhook (balloon), 23
Socorro (N.M.) incident, 68–71
Soter, Steven, 76
Soviet Union, 20, 28–29, 32, 33
Space Review, 62–63
Space World, 152
Spaulding, William H., 150
Steiger, Brad, 138, 142–43, 146–47
Sturrock, Peter A., 149
Sullivan, Walter, 112
Swamp-gas theory, 94–102, 116
Swann, Ingo, 138

Tassili drawings, 119–20
Temperature inversion, 39–40
Thy Kingdom Come (Green), 55
Time, 114
True, 43–44
Truman, Harry, 38
Tulli papyrus, 14–15
Two, the (Bo and Peep), 142–46

UFO Controversy in America, The (Jacobs), 18–19, 31
UFO Investigator, 151
UFOs—Yes! (Saunders and Harkins), 109
Uninvited Visitors (Sanderson), 132–33

Vallee, Jacques, 66–67, 131, 136, 138–41
Van Tassel, George, 55
Vegetable Man, 90–91
Virginia sighting, 35
von Däniken, Erich, 116–21

Wallace, Edgar, 54
Walton, Travis, 79–80
War of the Worlds (Wells), 44
Washington, D.C., "invasion" of, 36–41
Washington (state) sightings, 21, 24
Weather balloons, 26–27
Welles, Orson, 44
Wells, H. G., 44
West Virginia monsters, 87–91
When Prophecy Fails, 56
Whitted, John B., 25–26
World War II sightings, 19–20

XF-5-U-L (Flying Flapjack), 30

Zamora, Lonnie, 68–71